Intro

The beauty of the North Wales co ;,
has attracted visitors for many ye   1
of the Dee Estuary, the coastline exte -
ning scenery of great variety. This i. ____ ...pressive sand dunes, tidal
river estuaries, sand and shingle beaches, the limestone headlands of the
Great and Little Orme with their dramatic cliffs, the imposing mountains of
the northern Carneddau range tumbling to the sea, and the saltmarsh and
extensive mudflats of Traeth Lafan exposed at low tide stretching over
towards Anglesey.

The coast boasts a range of nature reserves and attracts many species of
birds, providing roosting and visiting sites of international importance. The
area also offers a wealth of important historical sites, monuments and buildings, ranging from pre-historic hillforts, burial and ceremonial sites to
medieval castles.

The best way to enjoy this diverse landscape and its birdlife, and appreci-
ate its history, is on foot, using the extensive network of good paths and
ancient trackways. The 20 circular walks in this book explore the coastline
and its adjoining unspoilt rural hinterland, including limestone hills and the
northern edges of the Carneddau mountains within the Snowdonia National
Park. They offer superb views and visit nature reserves and places of historical interest, including Rhuddlan and Deganwy Castles, Conwy medieval
town walls, and in more upland locations, remote Bronze Age standing
stones and 19thC telegraph stations.

The routes, which range from a 2¼ mile ramble through the dunes to a 7½
mile walk along the shoreline and across the Carneddau foothills, follow
public rights of way or permissive paths. Some utilise sections of the North
Wales Path. *A key feature is that many individual routes, as well as containing shorter walk options, can easily be linked to provide longer and more
challenging day walks, if required.* Be suitably equipped, especially on the
more exposed upland routes. Walking boots are recommended, along with
appropriate clothing to protect against the elements. Please remember that
the condition of paths can vary according to season and weather. Any path
problems encounted should be reported to the relevant Highways
Department. Each walk has a detailed map and description which enables
the route to be followed without difficulty, but be aware that changes in
detail can occur at any time. The location of each walk is shown on the back
cover and a summary of their key features is also given. This also includes an
estimated walking time, but allow more to enjoy the scenery. And please
always observe the country code.

Enjoy your walking!

WALK 1
POINT OF AYR

DESCRIPTION A 2¼ mile (**A**) or 1½ mile (**B**) walk featuring the impressive dunes of Talacre Warren and a 19thC lighthouse sited near the mouth of the treacherous Dee Estuary, internationally renowned for the waders and wildfowl it supports. Allow about 1¼ hours. The route offers an optional extension, or separate walk, of 1¼ miles along a small tidal inlet adjoining Point of Ayr Nature Reserve, an important roosting site for wetland birds, to visit an RSPB hide on the edge of the estuary. BHP Petroleum, who operate the nearby gas terminal which processes gas piped from platforms visible in Liverpool Bay, is involved with other agencies in a conservation programme for the area. Their advice was much appreciated. Respect any conservation work being undertaken.

START Talacre [SJ 124848]

DIRECTIONS Turn off the A548 coast road between Prestatyn and Holywell to reach Talacre. Park in the second signposted car park by the Smuggler's Inn.

Talacre Dunes, along with nearby Gronant Dunes, are the remnants of a dune system which once stretched along most of the North Wales coastline, and still serve as an important sea defence. The dunes and foreshore are a designated Special Site of Scientific Interest, being rich in plant, animal, bird and insect life. A notable landmark is the lighthouse built in 1819 to replace the original one established here in 1777. It had 4 floors and a blinking light with a range of 19 miles. It has survived a replacement 1844 iron tower, and a later tower built in 1891. Its subsequent uses have included a store, wartime lookout, and holiday home.

1 Go past the Smuggler's Inn and at the road end, turn LEFT through a kissing gate, signposted to Talacre Marsh. Go along

the concrete path, and at its end, bear LEFT along a wooden walkway. At a stony track, follow it RIGHT. The track passes through The Warren, an area rich in mixed vegetation with dunes on your right. After nearly ½ mile, turn RIGHT on a concrete path heading into the dunes.

2 Soon it splits. For **Walk A** take the LEFT fork and continue with a green path through the dunes. At its end, by a small clump of trees, follow the sandy path bearing half-LEFT. Ignore a path leading left, but continue ahead towards a post to pass between the tightly packed dunes. Keep on with the main path, soon swinging RIGHT over the high dunes to drop down onto the beach. Turn RIGHT to reach the lighthouse. (*For **Walk B**, take the RIGHT fork. When the path splits again, keep ahead, passing several side paths. At the end of the concrete path, follow the broad sandy path through the dunes ahead. After about 100 yards, with the main path bearing right, follow a path through the dunes to reach the beach. Turn RIGHT towards the lighthouse.*) Go past a waymark post on the beach.

3 After a further 300 yards, by a red lifebuoy stand, leave the beach at a waymarked access point. Go across open ground and up a wooden pathway to a viewing point. *From here you can look across the Dee*

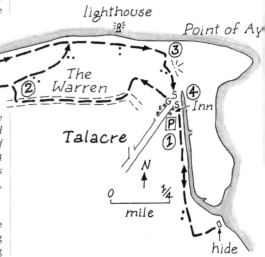

Estuary to the Wirral and Liverpool beyond. You may also see large ferries on route between Dublin and nearby Mostyn docks. Follow the raised walkway back to Talacre.

4 To visit the RSPB Hide continue along the embankment, passing a small wood, then the perimeter of BHP. Shortly follow a lower path below the tree-lined embankment to an old fence. Here, go LEFT to reach the large wooden RSPB hide.

WALK 2

GRONANT DUNES

DESCRIPTION A 2½ mile walk through Gronant Dunes, a designated Local Nature Reserve and Special Site of Scientific Interest. The dunes, extending east from a single narrow ridge into a series of parallel ridges, support a range of insects and plants, including the dominant marram grass, and less common species such as sea-holly, pyramidal orchid, sea and portland spurge. The foreshore and shingle attract a variety of birds, including wintering waders, cormorants and the only breeding colony of little terns in Wales. Allow about 1½ hours.
START Barkby Beach car park, Prestatyn [SJ 068840]
DIRECTIONS On the eastern outskirts of Prestatyn, turn off the A548 coast road into Marine Road East, signposted to Barkby beach. Go past Pontins, and on the bend near The Grand, enter the shoreline car park by Prestatyn Sailing Club.

1 From the car park walk east along a short section of promenade, then on a rough path above the shoreline. Take the next but one waymarked path up a wooden walkway to a viewing platform. Here turn LEFT and walk along the top of the dune ridge close by the fence. At its corner keep near the remaining section of fence, then follow a clear path ahead through the centre of the steadily widening dune system towards the distant Point of Ayr lighthouse – *initially enjoying good views over Barkby Beach*. After passing several side paths you reach a more open area and a crossroad of paths, with a view again to the sea.

2 Here, turn RIGHT and go up onto the dune ridge overlooking the golf course (*a small concrete tower here is due to be demolished*). Turn LEFT (or right for a shorter walk) and follow a clear path along the dune ridge, soon alongside the golf course wooden perimeter fence. At its end continue ahead past an old fence then a post, to emerge on a stony embanked cross path. Follow it LEFT to drop down on to an area containing a shallow lake (*it may be dry*). *Further east along the coast can be seen the high Talacre dunes.* Bear LEFT and follow a clear path alongside the dunes. Shortly, continue ahead between two lines of dunes to reach the crossroad of paths met earlier. Here, turn LEFT back up onto the dune ridge overlooking the golf course. Now turn

RIGHT and follow the path along the dune ridge – *with good views ahead of the mountains of Snowdonia and the Little Orme* – to join your outward route.

WALK 3

COED BELL & VOELNANT

DESCRIPTION A 4 mile (**A**) walk exploring the low hills at the northern end of the Clwydian Range AONB, offering extensive coastal views, and featuring a 19thC Telegraph Station and Coed Bell, an attractive area of mature deciduous woodland. Allow about 2½ hours. An alternative 3¼ mile walk (**B**), which extends the visit to Coed Bell, is described.

START Gronant Village Institute [SJ 092831]

DIRECTIONS Turn off the A548 Prestatyn-Holywell coast road signposted to Upper Gronant, and at a T-junction, turn left towards Llanasa. Just before the Gronant Inn, turn right up Nant y Crai lane. Take the first turning right passing between houses, to reach the Village Institute. Cars may be left in the large car park at the owner's risk. *The Institute was a gift from Richard Hughes, a Liverpool shipowner, to his native village in 1924.*

*O**n the open** hillside above Gronant stands Foel Nant – the former Voelnant Telegraph station and now a private house. It was one of a chain of 12 semaphore stations established by 1827 in prominent positions on Anglesey and along the North Wales coast providing an effective communication link between Holyhead and Liverpool. The purpose was to give merchants and shipowners in Liverpool early news of the arrival of their ships. The current building dates from 1841, when the Trustees of the Liverpool Docks provided each station with accommodation for the signalman and his family. The semaphore apparatus consisted of two masts, each fitted with 4 pivoting arms. Numbers used represented the alphabet and points of the compass. Signallers used a powerful telescope to constantly watch the next station in line. They became very skilled and able to relay signals at high speed. Apparently, during an official test in 1830, it took only 23 seconds to pass a message and reply between Liverpool and Holyhead!*

Unfortunately, they could not work at night or during bad weather, so about 1860, a new system of electrical transmission between five main stations was gradually introduced, and Voelnant and other intermediate stations closed down.

1 Walk back to the junction by the Gronant Inn. *The oldest part of the inn, now the lounge bar, dating from the early 18thC, was once a single storey shop called 'Central Buildings', providing everything from hardware items to bread baked in the bakehouse behind. It has also been a butcher's and chip shop.* Turn RIGHT past the Inn and follow the road through the village.After a few hundred yards, turn RIGHT up Pentre Lane, passing the old school. Just before Pentre farm, take the waymarked bridleway along a rough track, which soon rises past an old quarry. Keep with this delightful hedge/tree lined bridleway as it rises steadily up the hillside – *later offering good views to the coastal dunes, with the old Point of Ayr lighthouse prominent, and across the Dee Estuary to the Wirral and Liverpool beyond.* Eventually, the track levels out to reach a waymarked bridleway/path junction.

2 Here, swing RIGHT up a stony track and follow it to a large house. Continue ahead along a track, which soon becomes a path between boundaries. It heads west along the top edge of a line of low hills, passing a large walled enclosure. *This section offers extensive views seawards of gas-drilling platforms, and ships, including the regular Irish ferries. On a clear day the Lakeland Fells, Lancashire coast, Blackpool Tower, and the Pennines can be seen.* It bends past a pond, then shortly begins a gentle descent to reach a green track by a bridleway post and a large derelict house just ahead.

3 For **Walk B** bear RIGHT and follow the track down past woodland, then large barns and on down a lane. Just before a cottage, go over a stile on the left signposted to Coed Bell. Go up the slope ahead, over a stile in the fence corner, and on along the field edge. Cross a ladder-stile in the corner, then follow a path through Coed Bell. After about

4

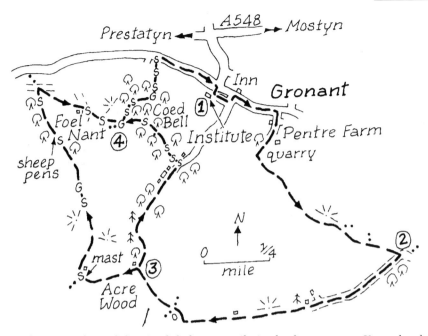

200 yards, ignore the path bearing left, but continue ahead through the trees on an indistinct path to cross a stile which you soon see ahead. Keep ahead to follow the fence on your right. After about 150 yards, go half-LEFT up a path through the bracken and gorse. Soon you reach a waymarked path junction by a wooden gate. Turn RIGHT and resume text at point **4**.

For **Walk A** turn LEFT and follow the gently rising track along the edge of Acre Wood. On the bend, by a Police transmitter mast, cross a stile on the right by a footpath post. Walk down the edge of the field alongside a fence on your right – *enjoying panoramic views.* The ground then levels out – *providing views west over Prestatyn and Rhyl, and along the coast to the Little Orme, Anglesey, and the northern Carneddau mountains.* Drop down to cross a stile and on through a gateway ahead. Shortly, descend the open hillside alongside a fence on your left, soon passing a small wood on your right. Just before sheep pens at the field bottom, bear RIGHT to cross a stile. Pass to the right of the sheep pens, by adjoining gates. Continue down through the right hand edge of the wood – with Foel Nant visible in the adjoining field – to cross

a stile in the fence corner. Keep ahead to work your way down through shrub and small trees to reach a track and a stile ahead by a small building. Turn RIGHT up the track, and after about 30 yards, head up the hillside towards Foel Nant. Pass the left-hand corner of its boundary wall to go over a waymarked stile just ahead. Now go half-RIGHT across the field to cross another stile. Go half-LEFT to follow a path passing close to gorse, and on between further gorse to reach a gated fence corner. Follow the fence on your left to go through a wooden gate by a waymarked path junction. Here, turn LEFT.

4 Drop down near the fence to cross a stile. Continue ahead down the field to cross a stile to enter Coed Bell. Follow the path down through the trees, to go through a double set of gates at the wood edge, and over the stile ahead. Continue down past the perimeter fence of Coed Bell cemetery to the road. Turn right along the road to Gronant. At the junction keep ahead, then turn RIGHT up steps, past a war memorial to return to the Institute. *A visit to the Gronant Inn makes a pleasant ending.*

5

Foryd Bridge

sea front

RHYL

Kinmel Bay

Marine lake

The Harbour

P

caravan site

River Clwyd

N

0   ¼

mile

visit the distinctive mound of Twt Hill – *occupying a command-ing position above the river Clwyd, with fine views down the Vale of Clwyd and along the Clwydian Hills.* Now go on to join the path which runs along the edge of a cara-van park and above the river Clwyd. It soon

Rhuddlan, lying beside an ancient crossing of the river Clwyd with access to the sea, is an important strategic and historical site. It was a key gateway offering the easiest access into the heartland of North Wales and for centuries was the focus of struggles between the Welsh and English. A motte and bailey castle was built in 1073 on Twt (look-out)Hill, reputedly on the site of an earlier Welsh stronghold. Nearby was a ditched Norman town, with its own priory. In 1277, Edward 1 chose an alternative nearby site for a new castle, com-pleted in 1281 – the first of several concen-tric castles he had built in North Wales - to reinforce his conquest campaigns. An impressive piece of medieval engineering was the conversion of the river into a deep water channel to facilitate improved seaborne access. A new town, which still forms the heart of Rhuddlan was built at the same time. In 1284, after the power of the Welsh had been broken, Edward held a Parliament at Rhuddlan, which set out the constitutional settlement for Wales in the 'statute of Rhuddlan' . In 1646, the castle was dismantled after being captured by General Mytton and the Parliamentarians.

1 From the car park, turn LEFT along the road, then just past a chapel, turn RIGHT along Cross Street. At the next junction, fol-low the road LEFT to reach Rhuddlan Castle. After visiting the castle, continue along Hylas Lane. After about 100 yards, by a house, bear RIGHT along a track on a path signposted to St.Asaph/Twt Hill, soon pass-ing a school playing field. After going through a kissing gate, continue ahead to

bears LEFT to cross a stile by a gate. Turn LEFT and follow the road passing the caravan park entrance, and hous-es, then take the first road on the left (Hylas Lane) Follow it past the school entrance and a thatched cottage back to the castle entrance. Go straight ahead back along Castle Street, and follow it past Tower House and the former National School (1829) to reach the High Street.

2 Cross the road and turn LEFT, then turn RIGHT along a lane, just before the bridges over the river, on the route of the North Wales Path. After passing beneath the attractive church of St. Mary's – *originally a single naved church founded about 1300 to serve the new town, but later a second nave and tower were added* – bear LEFT on a stony track and then cross a stile up to the left by a gate. Now follow a path along a flood embankment, passing under the Rhuddlan by-pass. Keep on with this path as

6

it follows the course of the river Clwyd towards the sea. *The estuary attracts a great variety of birds, including swans, herons, canadian geese, waders, cormorants, oyster catchers, gulls, and terns. According to tradition, it is also the site of battle in 795, when Caradoc, Prince of Gwynedd, and many of his Welsh supporters, were killed in battle by Offa, King of Mercia.* Eventually, the path veers away from the river to follow a large fence round to a waymarked path junction. Continue on the North Wales Path alongside the fence, through a kissing gate, and on along the perimeter of a caravan site. After going through another kissing gate, turn LEFT along a road to enter the suburbs of Rhyl. At a junction, bear half-LEFT across the road. (*For an optional extension back to the estuary, and a good stopping place to observe the birdlife, go through a kissing-gate and on along the Glan Morfa walkway. Take the left fork of the stony path, and continue over rough ground, then a track, past a waymark post to the estuary. Follow the estuary path towards the railway bridge and on back to the kissing-gate.*)

3 Go across the footbridge over the railway line and along a road. At the second set of crossroads, turn LEFT to reach the Marine Lake, with its boating and miniature railway. Bear RIGHT and follow the pathway round the edge of the lake. As you approach its north west corner, turn RIGHT with care over the miniature railway line and go past a gate, then bear LEFT along

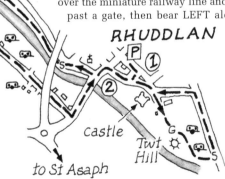

RHUDDLAN

castle

Twt Hill

to St Asaph

WALK 4
RHUDDLAN & CLWYD ESTUARY

DESCRIPTION A 6½ mile walk that combines Rhuddlan's notable sites of historical interest – a Norman fortress site, its massive 13thC stone castle, and medieval church – with a circuit of the nearby tidal Clwyd estuary – a birdwatcher's paradise! Binoculars are highly recommended. Allow about 3½ hours. It can easily be undertaken as two separate walks of 1 and 5½ miles.

START Car park opposite Rhuddlan Community Centre [SJ 024781] or Foryd Bridge, Rhyl [SH 995996]

DIRECTIONS On entering Rhuddlan from the St. Asaph direction, after crossing the river, go up the High Street, then just before the pelican crossing, turn right. You will find a car park on the left opposite the Community Centre. For the alternative start, Foryd Bridge lies on the A548 separating Kimnel Bay from the western end of Rhyl, where there are car parks.

the pavement. Go past the roundabout on the road signposted to Abergele to cross the Foryd Bridge over the river. *At the mouth of the estuary is a small harbour with a cluster of small boats, repair yards, and sand dunes.*

4 After crossing the bridge, take the first road on the left (Old Foryd Road). The road passes through a small new housing estate, and becomes Clwyd Bank. Follow it under the railway line, then immediately, bear LEFT up a track and go over a stile and on along the western flood embankment of the estuary The way back towards Rhuddlan, with its castle prominent in the distance, is obvious. Later a track runs alongside the embankment to eventually arrive at a caravan park. Continue along the lane, passing under the by-pass, to reach a road junction by Y Morfa restaurant bar. Turn LEFT and follow the road towards Rhuddlan, soon crossing the footbridge over the river alongside the ancient stone road bridge. Continue up the High Street back to the start.

WALK 5

CWM DULAS & GOPA WOOD

DESCRIPTION A 7 mile walk exploring the coast and unspoilt rural hinterland between Abergele and Llanddulas, with good views. The route starts with a 2½ walk along the shoreline following the North Wales Path between Pensarn and Llanddulas, then heads inland up the hidden Dulas valley, before skirting one of the limestone hills which dominate the valley. It then follows field paths to explore an attractive wooded hill, managed by the Woodland Trust. Allow about 4 hours.

START Pensarn beach [SH 942786]

DIRECTIONS At Pensarn on the A548 Rhyl-Abergele coast road, go over the railway by Abergele & Pensarn station, and follow the road left to the third car park by the promenade.

1 Walk west along the promenade up to an information board. From here the route follows the coastal cycle/walkway to Llandulas. (For an alternative initial section, head over to the shore and follow a stony path above the pebble beach.) *There are fine views along the coast to the Little Orme. Inland, set amongst the densely wooded hillside, stands the picturesque Gwrych Castle – an extensive folly. The gothic castellated mansion, with its towers and walls, was built in 1819-22 for Lloyd Bamford Hesketh.* After about ½ mile the cycle/walkway runs close by the shoreline, passes a series of groynes, then The Beachcomber and a caravan site. Later it passes the Afon Dulas where it enters the sea, then crosses a bridge over the river.

2 Just before a road, by the old lifeboat house, bear LEFT alongside the river. Go under the railway and A55 bridges, then bear LEFT along Beach road. It soon crosses over the river, and goes on past houses to reach the main road in Llanddulas. (*For refreshments turn right to the Valentine Inn.*) Turn LEFT then RIGHT along Beaulah Avenue past the stylish village hall. After passing an

attractive converted 19thC church, continue along Bryn Dulas road, passing over the river and on up to a small junction by a house. Continue ahead on this delightful quiet shady road south along Cwm Dulas, passing beneath the densely wooded slopes of Craig y Forwyn. Soon, it descends to another junction. Take the LEFT fork down Cwymp road and keep ahead at the next junction. Follow the road over the river, and on past the attractive Cwymp Mill. *Just beyond look across the valley to the impressive limestone escarpment of Craig y Forwyn (Maiden's Leap) – with its tales of a local girl's spurned love and suicide.* Continue up the road.

3 On the next bend, turn RIGHT past a cottage on an access track. After about 25 yards, take a waymarked path angling off the track through the trees. After crossing a stile, keep on with the path to pass below houses to reach a road at Rhyd-y-foel. Turn LEFT, then cross a stile on the right opposite the

8

first cottage. Follow the path straight ahead to bear LEFT, then RIGHT to rise through the trees to a fence beneath open

slopes and the impressive limestone crags of Pen-y-corddyn-mawr – *on which are the remains of a 37 acre 1st century AD. hillfort.* Here, swing RIGHT on a green path. After about 50 yards take its LEFT fork up to join a delightful path rising across the western shrub-covered scree slopes – *enjoying extensive views to the mountains of Snowdonia.*

The path soon levels out and upon leaving an area of gorse, go through a gap in the old tree boundary corner just ahead. Follow the boundary on your right, which soon bears left, then drop through a large gap in the boundary corner near a small ruin. Drop down the slope onto the green track below, and follow it LEFT to cross a stile. Follow the track down, and when it bends right, keep straight ahead to walk alongside the tree boundary on your right, with the wooded limestone crags up to your left.

4 At the site of an old well, ignore the path leading to a field, but follow a path on the inside of the tree boundary to pass behind houses. Keep close to the fence to go through a gate and drop down onto the driveway by an outbuilding. Follow the waymarked path half-RIGHT across the yard to go through a gate at the end of another outbuilding. Keep ahead, through another gate, and on along the field edge to cross a stile. Continue ahead and at the hedge corner, angle towards a stile in the boundary ahead. Go half-RIGHT down to cross a stile onto a lane. Go over the stile opposite and along the field edge to cross a gate in the corner. Keep ahead for about 70 yards, then go half-LEFT up to a wood corner. Go along the edge of Betws Lodge Wood, passing through a gateway, and on by a large field. Go through a gate in the top field corner, and on towards a farm. Pass between buildings, then turn LEFT to pass in front of the house, before swinging RIGHT along its access track.

5 When it bends right, cross a stile just ahead to enter Gopa Wood. Go up the path to a green track, and follow it LEFT. Soon, when it splits, take the RIGHT fork angling through the trees. At a waymarked path junction, continue straight ahead. The path soon drops down LEFT by a path junction, to cross a footbridge over a narrow ravine. It continues on a steady descent before bearing RIGHT more steeply down onto a track. (*For splendid views go left and up to the right on the bend*). Turn RIGHT and follow the stony track down to a waymarked path junction by two seats at another good viewpoint. Swing sharp LEFT down the track, and, shortly, as it begins to bend, drop down a long stepped path on your right to leave the wood by a seat and road junction on the edge of Abergele. Go RIGHT down the road, past the golf club entrance, then go LEFT along Ffordd Tan'r allt. Follow it to the A547 by the main entrance to Gwrych Castle. Follow it RIGHT towards Abergele centre, then go LEFT along Sea Road. Follow it over the A55 and railway line to reach your starting point.

9

WALK 6

MYNYDD MARIAN

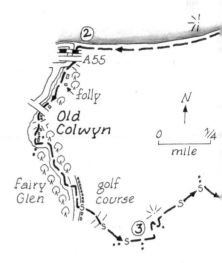

DESCRIPTION A 7¼ mile walk that combines an interesting section of coastline, with the attractive limestone countryside between Old Colwyn and Llanddulas, incorporating sections of the North Wales Path. The route follows the coast before heading inland via Fairy Glen up to Mynydd Marian, a small limestone ridge nature reserve by Llysfaen, featuring an early 19thC telegraph station and offering extensive views. It returns down the attractive Dulas valley with its impressive limestone escarpments. Allow about 4 hours. An alternative return via road to Llanddulas provides a 6 mile circuit.

START Shoreline car park, Llanddulas [SH 907786]

DIRECTIONS Leave the A55 for Llanddulas and follow signs for the beach to reach the shoreline parking area and toilets.

1 Follow the cycle/walkway west along the shoreline towards Colwyn Bay – *with fine views along the coast to the Little Orme.* It passes close to the railway line and the A55, before passing two conveyor belt carrying jetties. *For centuries, limestone from the nearby Llanddulas/Llysfaen quarries has been transported by sea from here to various places in Britain and overseas. In the 18thC, small single masted flat bottomed barges were beached and loaded from horse drawn carts. In the 19th C, wooden jetties were built to accommodate sailing sloops, and later the famous Gem line of steamers, each named after a precious stone, which operated until the 1930's. Before the introduction of conveyor belts which enabled stone to be moved directly from the quarry to ships, loading was provided by teams of men, working to the tide. Nowadays, ships still berth alongside the second 660 foot jetty, arriving 3 hours before high tide and leaving within 1 hour of high tide occurring.* Continue along the cycle/walkway on past a small rocky headland.

2 Just before a road, you leave the coast, by turning LEFT to go under the railway and

A55 bridges. Cross the road and follow the waymarked North Wales Path path alongside the stream, past cottages, ignoring side paths, to pass through an underpass at Old Colwyn. Continue ahead alongside the stream past cottages. Soon, go half-LEFT up a stepped path, then bear RIGHT (Fairy Glen) past more cottages. Keep ahead past Awelon to rejoin the stream in a wood. Just before a footbridge, swing LEFT to follow the path through the wooded valley above the stream. At a road, turn RIGHT and after about 120 yards, turn LEFT on the North Wales path. Follow it half-RIGHT up across the golf course to go through a gateway in the corner. Go half-RIGHT across a lane to cross the stile ahead. Follow the hedge on your left up to reach an enclosed track. Follow it LEFT.

3 Shortly, leave the North Wales Path by continuing ahead on the track signposted to Marian Bach. Near the top of the rise, bear LEFT, passing a small rock face. Just beyond, the faint track ends. Continue ahead to the field corner, then swing RIGHT along the field edge and on over a stile in the corner to a waymarked path junction. Turn RIGHT along an enclosed path, and, after crossing a stile, bear half-LEFT to walk alongside an old wall. Soon cross a ladder-stile and go past the end of two large corrugated barns, then go RIGHT along the side of the second one. Keep ahead, past the complex of Ty Mawr to

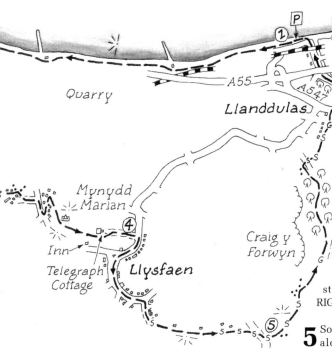

another junction, keep ahead, and just beyond the next bend, turn RIGHT at a way-mark post signposted Bryn Defaid to rejoin the North Wales Path. Follow the stony track, and just past the entrance to Bryn Celyn, cross a stile up on your left. Walk along the limestone ridge, with the wall to your left. At the wall end, keep ahead, parallel with an access track, soon passing beneath a small caravan park. After a stile below a house, go past the far end of a breeze-block building and on to cross a stile. After another stile, turn RIGHT along an access track.

5 Soon cross a ladder-stile and go along a green track. After 100 yards, when it bears half-right, continue straight ahead to a waymark post beneath a wall, and on up to cross a stile. Now go half-RIGHT up the slope ahead and on to cross a ladder-stile. Follow the clear path heading up towards the crags of Craig y Forwyn (Maiden's Leap) – *with its tales of a local girl's spurned love and suicide.* After 100 yards, keep on the right fork, and after another 50 yards, at a faint cross path, bear RIGHT along a side ridge, soon dropping down to a waymark post. The path now descends steadily beneath the impressive limestone crags and scree slopes into the wooded valley. At a road, cross the stile opposite. Follow the path down the field and on along the edge of this and the next field. Go through a kissing gate and on down a lane, then enclosed path to reach the centre of Llandulas, by the Valentine Inn. Cross the road and turn RIGHT past St. Cynbryd's church, then turn LEFT along a side road. The road crosses the river and soon reaches a junction by the A55 road bridge. Turn RIGHT along by the river, go under the railway bridge and turn LEFT back to the start.

go down a concrete track, below the last house. Just past the outbuilding on your right, turn RIGHT along a path and on along the access track to the road. Turn RIGHT and after 150 yards, swing sharp LEFT past Anneddle. Keep with the main track, and at Rose Villa, swing RIGHT up onto Mynyndd Marian to reach its summit with trig point and enclosed sunken reservoir. Pass to the right of the metal fence, then bear LEFT on a path along the top edge of an old quarry and on past another covered reservoir and Telegraph cottage. *This was one of a chain of 12 semaphore stations established between Holyhead and Liverpool by 1827 to give merchants and shipowners early news of the arrival of their ships. (See* **Walk 3** *for more details)* Just beyond its garden corner wall, bear half-LEFT and follow its access track to the road.

4 Turn RIGHT. (*For the shorter walk, follow the road left down into Llanddulas.*) At a road junction, bear LEFT (*or continue ahead for refreshments at the Castle Inn.*) At the next junction continue straight ahead. At

WALK 7

BRYN EURYN

DESCRIPTION A 7½ mile (**A**) walk, offering panoramic views, that meanders through the attractive undulating countryside bordering Mochdre, Colwyn Bay and Rhos-on-Sea, linking 4 designated Countryside Sites and a Woodland Trust site. The route rises from Mochdre to cross the hillside, appropriately named The View, visits Bryn Cadno nature reserve, then descends into an attractive side valley. It continues through the ancient woodland of Coed Pwllycrochan, before heading north to explore Bryn Euryn, a limestone hill nature reserve, SSSI, and the site of an ancient hillfort. It then heads west to follow a low ridge to pass by attractive woodland. Allow about 4½ hours. The route offers shorter walks of 2 miles (**B**), and 5 miles (**C**). Alternatively, you can follow a waymarked 1 mile Summit Trail of Bryn Euryn from the reserve's car park, passing the ruins of Llys Euryn, a 15thC fortified mansion, or use it to link into the main route.
START Old Conway Road, Mochdre [SH 826786] or Bryn Euryn Nature Reserve [SH 835802]
DIRECTIONS Follow the A547 through Mochdre, and near a pelican crossing by shops, take a side road signposted Phoenix Workshops/P to find a car park on the right. For Bryn Euryn Reserve, follow Rhos road from the promenade in Rhos-on-Sea, to its end.

1 Cross the A547 and go along Old Conway Road opposite, then turn LEFT up Singleton Crescent. At a junction, turn LEFT and follow the road up the hillside. Go past the entrance to a caravan park, then turn RIGHT over a stile by Thornhurst, signposted Hafoty Lane, and on over another stile. Go up the field and after about 125 yards, head half-RIGHT to go through the top field corner. Continue up a path by a fence to reach a superb viewpoint: *views include Conwy castle, river and mountain, the northern Carneddau, Anglesey, Puffin Island, the Great and Little Orme, and Bryn Euryn.*

Continue alongside the fence, go over two stiles and follow the path up across The View to cross a stile in the fence corner, and on to reach a track by a house.

2 Turn LEFT along the track. (*Shortly, for* **Walk B**, *cross a stile on the left and follow the waymarked path along the edge of 4 fields to join your outward route*). Follow the track then lane to reach Mynydd Lane. Follow it LEFT, and at a road junction, turn RIGHT, then take the second turning on the left – Honeysuckle Lane. Just past Fir Tree cottage enter Bryn Cadno nature reserve on the left. Follow the path across the hillside up to a picnic table to enjoy extensive views. Retrace your steps and continue along the lane. At its end follow a delightful hedge/tree-lined path down to a road. Turn LEFT and follow this quiet country road down the edge of the attractive Nant y Groes valley, and up past Gwern-Tyno farm.

3 At the entrance to Fox Hill house, take the waymarked path angling up through the trees, and follow it through the edge of mature woodland to reach a stony access track. Turn RIGHT down the track and on down a lane. Just before a junction is an information board on Coed Pwllycrochan. Here enter the wood, and at a waymarked path junction, take the RIGHT fork to follow the orange route contouring the wooded slopes to eventually descend to another information board by the road. Continue on the orange route to the bend of the road by a stream, and back up into the wood. When the orange route turns left, continue ahead along the wood edge above the road to cross the B5113 at crossroads. Continue along the wood edge to another crossroads.

4 Turn RIGHT. (*For* **Walk C**, *go up Old Highway opposite, past the zoo, and on down to join your outward route.*) Follow Llanwrst Road down, past junctions, to the A547. Cross the road and go across the footbridge over the A55 and railway. Cross a stile by a footpath post, and follow the path along the bottom edge of the wood, soon rising alongside a fence to run parallel with the railway/A55. At a waymark post, swing

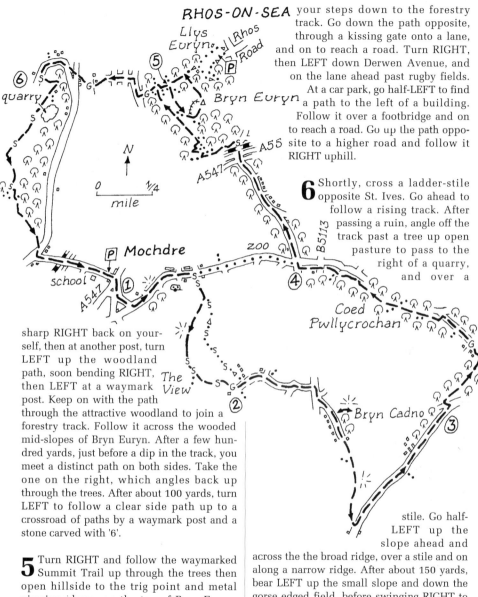

RHOS-ON-SEA
Llys Euryn
Rhos Road
P
Bryn Euryn
A55
A547
quarry
6
5
N
0   ¼
mile
Mochdre
P
school
A547
1
ZOO
B5113
4
Coed Pwllycrochan
The View
2
Bryn Cadno
3

your steps down to the forestry track. Go down the path opposite, through a kissing gate onto a lane, and on to reach a road. Turn RIGHT, then LEFT down Derwen Avenue, and on the lane ahead past rugby fields. At a car park, go half-LEFT to find a path to the left of a building. Follow it over a footbridge and on to reach a road. Go up the path opposite to a higher road and follow it RIGHT uphill.

6 Shortly, cross a ladder-stile opposite St. Ives. Go ahead to follow a rising track. After passing a ruin, angle off the track past a tree up open pasture to pass to the right of a quarry, and over a

sharp RIGHT back on yourself, then at another post, turn LEFT up the woodland path, soon bending RIGHT, then LEFT at a waymark post. Keep on with the path through the attractive woodland to join a forestry track. Follow it across the wooded mid-slopes of Bryn Euryn. After a few hundred yards, just before a dip in the track, you meet a distinct path on both sides. Take the one on the right, which angles back up through the trees. After about 100 yards, turn LEFT to follow a clear side path up to a crossroad of paths by a waymark post and a stone carved with '6'.

stile. Go half-LEFT up the slope ahead and across the the broad ridge, over a stile and on along a narrow ridge. After about 150 yards, bear LEFT up the small slope and down the gorse edged field, before swinging RIGHT to cross a stone stile by an old gate into a wood. Turn LEFT and follow a path down near the fence to reach a cross-path. Ignore a stile, but turn LEFT to follow the delightful enclosed path along the edge of the wood down to the road. Turn RIGHT, then LEFT along Station Road back into Mochdre.

5 Turn RIGHT and follow the waymarked Summit Trail up through the trees then open hillside to the trig point and metal viewing plaque on the top of Bryn Euryn. *Here are remains of a fort, known as Dineirth – the 'bear's fort' – reputed to be the stronghold of Cynlas Goch, the local ruler in the 6thC.* Head down towards Rhos-on-Sea to follow the Summit Trail down the steep open slopes and through the trees to a broad cross-path. Follow it LEFT and soon retrace

WALK 8
THE LITTLE ORME & COED GAER

DESCRIPTION A 5 mile figure of eight walk of contrasting coast and inland scenery, with great views. The route visits the small limestone headland of the Little Orme, with its cliffs and seabirds, before exploring the adjoining attractive low limestone hills and woodland. Allow about 3 hours. It can easily be undertaken as two separate walks of 2 and 3 miles respectively.

START Penrhyn-side [SH 814818]

DIRECTIONS Leave Llandudno on the B5115 towards Penrhyn Bay. Follow the road up past Craigside Manor, and at the top of the hill, just before it descends to a dual carriageway, turn right into Bryn y Bia road. Just beyond a bus shelter is a small off-road parking area on the left. Alternatively, turn left into Pendre road, where there is parking by Penrhyn-side village hall up on the right.

The Little Orme is part of a line of limestone extending from Anglesey along the North Wales coast and south to Llangollen, formed from marine life over 320 million years ago when this area was a tropical sea. It has been a site of great archaelogical importance since Neolithic times. A Site of Special Scientific Interest, it is home to a variety of sea and land birds, including kittiwakes, guillemots, cormorants, razor-bills, little terns, shags, and peregrine falcon, and contains many unusual plants. It includes Rhiwledyn Nature Reserve managed by the North Wales Wildlife Trust. In the 1580's, one of its caves housed a printing press, which secretly produced Catholic prayers, poetry and other manuscripts. Between 1889 to 1931, limestone was extensively quarried on the seaward side, from where it was shipped for use in blast furnaces in Scotland, and later in the manufacture of Portland cement. The site had its own narrow gauge railway and crushing plant. Between 1941-44, an Artillery practice camp was based here, providing essential training in night firing.

1 Return to the B5115 and follow it LEFT down towards Llandudno. Cross the road and shortly go through a kissing gate by an emergency telephone. Follow the way-marked North Wales Path RIGHT past an information board. It winds steadily up and across the slopes of the Little Orme. After going through a kissing gate, leave the North Wales Path and bear half-RIGHT to walk up alongside a hedge/tree old boundary and on past small crags to reach the distinct stone corner of the old boundary – *with views across the bay to the Great Orme and Llandudno.* Here swing LEFT and head up to the trig point on the summit of the Little Orme. *Enjoy the superb view in both directions along the coast, and to the mountains of Snowdonia.* Retrace your steps back down to the kissing gate. Continue with the North Wales Path, soon descending through gorse and bracken to reach a dramatic viewpoint overlooking the old quarry. Turn RIGHT.

2 Follow the waymarked path as it winds its way down into the quarry basin to reach the concrete remains of a winding gantry. Go through the small gate and down the incline to reach a footpath post. A short diversion LEFT will provide you with a good view of the cliffs with nesting birds and a small inlet. Return to the footpath post and walk past fenced-off sections where the cliffs have been eroded, and on along a stony path to the left of a worked out depression, past an information board. Just beyond, the path splits. Leave the North Wales Path and continue along the stony path. When it splits again, keep ahead to go through a kissing gate onto a lane past houses. Just past the second house, swing sharp RIGHT through a hidden kissing gate. Go up the path, soon take the LEFT fork, and go on through a farm. Follow its access track to the B5115. Turn LEFT and return to Bryn y Bia road.

3 Go up Pendre road, and just past the war memorial, take a stepped path on the right and go on up to a lane. Turn RIGHT, then go LEFT on a track behind Mount Pleasant terrace. Soon cross a stile on the right, go on up the field and through a kissing gate. Turn LEFT, then near the large wall corner, bear half-RIGHT through gorse just beneath the summit of Mynydd Pant – *from where there are extensive views* – to a way-marked fence corner. Follow the boundary on your left, along a hedge-lined path and on through a small gate. At a lane, follow it RIGHT – *with good views across Llandudno to the Great Orme*. On the bend, take

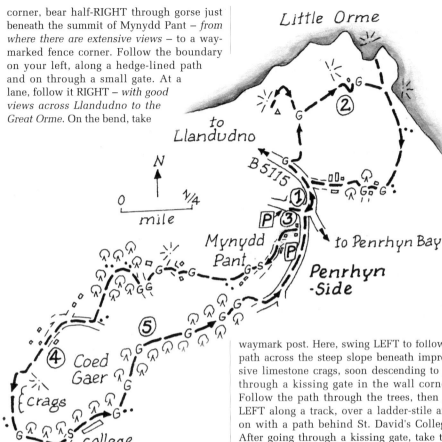

the waymarked bridleway ahead to reach a metalled track. Go through the gate opposite and follow the path through the wood, soon taking the LEFT fork, rising steadily through the trees. Shortly, go half-LEFT up another path, emerging from the wood onto a small limestone hill. Follow the hedge on your right to a lane. Turn RIGHT along the lane, and at a lane/track junction, turn LEFT along a track past Tan-y-Coed cottage.

4 At the track end, continue up open ground to the left of a garage and on alongside the hedge on your right, through a narrow enclosed section to reach a superb viewpoint. Follow the path down to a way-mark post – *with a good view of Conwy Castle* – then bear RIGHT down to another

waymark post. Here, swing LEFT to follow a path across the steep slope beneath impressive limestone crags, soon descending to go through a kissing gate in the wall corner. Follow the path through the trees, then go LEFT along a track, over a ladder-stile and on with a path behind St. David's College. After going through a kissing gate, take the LEFT of two waymarked paths, rising steadily alongside the wood edge. Go through a kissing gate and on up through Coed Gaer.

5 Leave the wood by a kissing gate, and turn RIGHT. Follow the wall to go through another kissing gate in the wall corner. Continue alongside the wall, through a kissing gate, then bear half-LEFT through the trees. After passing through a small clearing, continue on through two further kissing gates. At the wood edge go through another kissing gate and down an enclosed path between houses, across a track to reach a lane by a chapel. Follow it to a junction, then bear LEFT along the main street of the small community of Penrhyn-side, passing the Cross Keys and Penrhyn Arms, back to the start.

WALK 9
THE GREAT ORME (EAST)

DESCRIPTION An exploration of the eastern section of the Great Orme, offering two alternative circuits: a 3¾ mile walk (**A**) and a 3¼ mile walk (**B**). Both share the outward path, visiting the historically interesting hill of Pen Dinas on route to the12thC St. Tudno's church. **Walk A** continues to the summit with its cafe, visitor centre and extensive views, then passes the old copper mines on its inland return. **Walk B** takes a seaward return via Marine Drive for some delightful coastal scenery. Allow about 2½ hours. **Walk A** can also be undertaken from the Summit car park, starting from point **5**, missing out the ascent/descent through Happy Valley.
START Cenotaph, northern end of the North Shore Promenade, Llandudno [SH 782826] or Summit car park for **Walk A** alternative start [SH 766833].

*T**he Great Orme** is an impressive Carboniferous limestone headland, formed from the remains of small sea creatures once living in the tropical sea which covered the area about 350 million years ago. A Site of Special Scientific Interest, and managed as a Country Park and Nature Reserve, it contains many sites of historical and archaelogical interest. Its famous feral Kashmir goats, said to originate from a pair sent with others from India as a present for Queen Victoria, have been roaming wild since the 1890's. Nearby is the elegant Victorian seaside resort of Llandudno, largely built between 1850 – 1912. A unique cable-hauled tramway, has carried visitors from the town to the summit (679 feet/207 metres) since 1903. Marine Drive is a spectacular toll road, which opened in 1878, to replace a path, which Prime Minister William Gladstone complained about during a visit in 1868. It offers the best close views of the stunning cliff scenery and its many seabirds, and is incorporated in both **Walks 9 & 10**.*

1 From the Cenotaph, walk to the Grand Hotel, built in 1901. Here take the road signposted to the cable car/ski slope. *The nearby iron pier was built in 1876/7.* Soon bear LEFT with the road up through Happy Valley. Just past the toilet, take the walkway to your right parallel to the road. After going through a kissing gate, turn RIGHT, then LEFT up steps to follow the waymarked 'Summit Trail' through the attractive terraced gardens. When you reach steps leading to a small wooden gate at its top right hand corner, turn LEFT past a large stone shelter and cross the road to go through a metal gate opposite.

2 Follow the main path parallel to the road, passing above an information board. At a waymark post, turn sharp LEFT to follow the path to the southerly side of the summit of Pen Dinas. *This area is a Scheduled Ancient Monument containing many features of archaelogical interest, and is the site of an Iron Age fort. The stone with the plaque 'Rocking Stone' ('Maen Sigl') is reputed to have been used by druids in dealing with people accused of certain acts. The person stood on the stone, and only if it rocked, was he/she declared innocent!* Retrace your steps to the bottom of the slope, then bear LEFT along another path to reach a lane. Follow it RIGHT past the Alpine Lodge and the adjoining dry ski slopes. Continue on a waymarked path, through a kissing gate and on by the toboggan run to reach a cross-path by seats. Follow it LEFT up steps.

3 At a waymark post, take the path signposted to 'St. Tudno's church' Keep to the waymarked 'Summit Trail' path, and just before Pink Farm, go through a kissing gate. Go past the farm buildings and on along a track, then path, through a kissing gate to reach Ffynnon Powell. *Folklore says this spring miraculously appeared after a farmer named Powell and his family prayed for God's intervention at St. Tudno's church during a time of severe drought, when they were refused access to the area's wells.* Soon you reach the road by St. Tudno's church. *The church was named after Tudno, a 6thC Christian who built the first church in the*

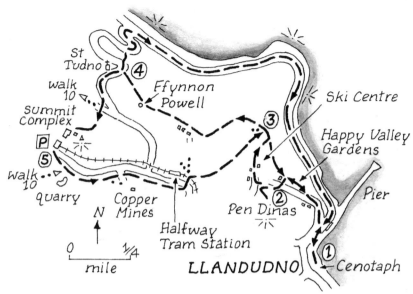

area, and after whom Llandudno (meaning 'enclosure of Tudno') was named.

4 For **Walk B** turn RIGHT then take a way-marked path, which meanders down to rejoin the road. Follow the road down to the junction with Marine Drive, which you then follow east. As you turn the corner, views across to the Little Orme appear, followed by the pier and the splendid frontage of Llandudno. The limestone cliffs tower above you, alive to the sound of nesting birds. *You pass a series of arches, formed by stone extraction. Go past the toll-gate, the Happy Valley Gardens and on back to the start.)*

For **Walk A** follow the road LEFT and after passing a multi-waymark post bear half-RIGHT across open ground, over a stony track to follow the waymarked trail to the summit. *The present complex was built as a hotel in 1903, and the surrounding area was developed as a golf course. The hotel was once owned by Randolf Turpin, the then world middleweight boxing champion. It is the terminus of both the tramway and the cable car, built in 1969. During the 19thC, a semaphore station, one of a chain built by Liverpool Dock Trustees, operated here, transmitting messages beween between*

Holyhead and Liverpool. *(See* **Walk 3** *for more details). From the trig point there are extensive views.*

5 From the road beneath the summit com-plex head down a path towards the quar-ry opposite, then bear LEFT to follow a way-marked path by a fence. At a waymark post, go half-LEFT signposted 'Ski Llandudno', across the access road to the Copper Mines, and on with a waymarked path near the road. Go past a road junction and the half-way tramway station, then go LEFT across the road and tramway just before they bend down to the right. Now go RIGHT up a way-marked stony track, which soon bears left passing under cables to drop gently down to reach the waymarked path junction met at point 3. Follow the stepped path down and continue ahead across the exposed limestone slope, passing seats. Follow the stepped path down to go through a wooden gate to drop down into Happy Valley Gardens. *(For those starting from the Summit car park, turn right past a stone shelter to cross the road and go through a metal gate opposite. Now follow instructions from point 2.)* Follow your out-ward route back down through the gardens to the start.

WALK 10

THE GREAT ORME (WEST)

DESCRIPTION A 6½ mile walk (**A**) exploring the splendid coastal scenery and upland limestone countryside to be found on the western half of the Great Orme. Allow about 3½ hours. The route offers an alternative finish making for a 5½ mile walk (**B**)
START Gogarth Abbey Hotel, West Shore, Llandudno [SH 769822] Road parking nearby. Alternatively the Summit car park [SH 766853]
For information on The Great Orme see **Walk 9**.

1 Follow the road past the hotel, and just beyond the castellated stone toll house, turn RIGHT through a kissing gate. After a few yards, at a footpath post bear LEFT on a rising path, passing beneath heavily eroded cliffs. *To the west is a stunning view across the bay to Conwy and Carneddau mountains, along the coast to Llanfairfechan, and across to Anglesey and Puffin Island.* Soon the path drops down to pass alongside a wall, before continuing along a lane behind houses to join Marine Drive. The road rises steadily beneath limestone buttresses, offering great seaward views. *Folklore has it that the sea hides the legendary lands of Helig which disappeared under the waters in the 6thC. After a while, you will see below the remains of an area known as the Gunsite, where the Royal Artillery ran Officer Cadet courses in gunnery, wireless and searchlight skills during the Second World War. At its peak, this peaceful green coastal site housed over 700 people.* Shortly, the road levels out and bends towards Pen-y-Gogarth (Great Orme's Head), soon passing Ffynnon Gaseg – *a well that doubtless once serviced the passing horse-drawn traffic.*

2 Just before the next bend, opposite a rising concrete track, a waymarked Nature Trail path gives good views of the high cliffs. Continue along the road, past the Rest and Be Thankful Cafe to the entrance to The Great Orme's Head Lighthouse. *This castel-lated two-storey building, designed by Chief Engineer of the Mersey Docks and Harbour Board and set high on the steep cliffs, served as a lighthouse from 1862 until 1985, after which it became a unique bed and breakfast establishment. It said to be haunted by the ghost of Austin, a former lighthouse keeper, who drowned trying to save a mariner. The road makes a steady descent through the dramatic landscape of limestone crags and steep cliffs with their many seabirds. Out to sea you may catch sight of the ferries travelling between Liverpool and Ireland. After a while look back for an excellent view of the lighthouse perched high on the towering cliffs.* At the 'Vehicle No Entry' sign, by a toll booth, swing sharp RIGHT up a zig-zag road. At a footpath post, take a meandering path up the hillside to rejoin the road. Continue along the road St. Tudno's church. *Dating from the 12th C, this neat church was named after Tudno, a 6thC Christian who built the first church in the area, and after whom Llandudno (meaning 'enclosure' of Tudno) was named.* After passing a multi-waymark post bear RIGHT across open ground to reach a stony track.

3 Turn RIGHT and follow the track across the hillside, soon alongside a large wall to pass Ffynnon Rhufeinig (*the Roman Well – although its connection with the Romans is uncertain*). The track becomes increasingly green as it heads across a delightful plateau of limestone walls, pavement, and meadows, with occasional large rock glacial erratics. Keep alongside the wall until you reach a distinct wall corner. Here, turn LEFT, still keeping the wall on your left, soon passing an area of limestone pavements. After a while, a waymark post leads you to a small stone cairn at a superb viewpoint. Continue ahead. As the land gently descends, you reach two Nature Trail waymark posts. (*For* **Walk B** *take the path leading down half-RIGHT. Known as Monk's Path, from its reputed use by monks in the past, this delightful descent will take you to the road. Follow it back to the start.*) For **Walk A**, continue ahead on a clear green path, still with the wall on your left. Eventually at the wall corner, head half-LEFT, soon passing a quar-

Great Orme's Head
lighthouse

Pen-y-Gogarth

café

Ffynnon Gaseg

limestone pavements

Ffynnon Rufeinig

summit complex

St Tudno's

walk 9

walk 9

copper mines

walk 9

P

Marine Drive

quarry

cromlech

N

0 ¼ mile

West Shore lake

Hotel

LLANDUDNO

to walk 11

ry. *A short diversion takes you to the nearby summit complex, with its Visitor Centre, café and extensive views.*

4 From the quarry follow the track almost to the road, then continue on a way-marked path by a fence, at first parallel with the road, towards the Copper Mines – *whose earliest workings date from the Bronze Age, some 4,000 years ago. It is believed to be the most extensive copper mine of the ancient world.* At a split access lane, ignore the one to the Mines unless you wish to visit. Instead, turn RIGHT past the entrance to a house and on with a stony track passing behind the mine buildings, through a gate and past houses, soon becoming Pyllau Road. At a junction, turn RIGHT, then short-ly turn RIGHT into Cromlech Road. At its end cross a stile to view the Cromlech – *a Neolithic Burial Chamber, dating from 3,500-2,500 BC., known as Llety'r Filiast (the hair of the greyhound bitch).* Return to the junc-tion and turn RIGHT along the road.

5 At the wall corner of Baron Hill, turn LEFT down past a converted chapel. Go down a stepped path, then bear LEFT to a road by a junction. Swing RIGHT along Tyn-y-Coed road. Follow it past houses to its end by Anglesea Road at a fine viewpoint. Go through a kissing gate and go half-RIGHT on a path. After about 100 yards, drop down a stepped path. Ignore cross-paths and follow the impressive stone stepped zig-zag path down the steep open hillside – *enjoying the final panoramic views* – to a tarmac path by a stone shelter. Follow it RIGHT to the road near the start.

WALK 11
DEGANWY CASTLE

DESCRIPTION A 5¼ mile walk between Llandudno and Deganwy, featuring two sites of historical interest – an old watchtower and the ruins of Deganwy Castle, an excellent section of coast from the mouth of the Conwy estuary to West Shore in Llandudno, and extensive views. Allow about 3 hours.

START Southern end of West Parade, West Shore, Llandudno. [SH 774815]

DIRECTIONS If travelling on the A546 from Deganwy, cross the railway line at the outskirts of Llandudno, then, after passing North Wales Golf Club, at crossroads, turn left into Trinity Crescent. Follow the road round to turn left along Dale Road to reach the southern end of West Parade, where there is a car park/roadside parking.

The twin hills above Deganwy, which have probably been occupied since Roman times, have witnessed centuries of settlement and warfare. During the 6th and 9th centuries, a castle built in 517 for Maelgwyn Gwynedd, occupied this site. In 1078, a new Norman castle was built here by Robert of Rhuddlan. During the 13th C Deganwy was a focus of the campaigns by the English Kings to exert control over Wales. In 1215, the castle was rebuilt by Llywelyn ap Iorwerth after successfully regaining land lost to King John, and after some years of peace, it withstood a siege by Henry III in 1245, but by 1257 was in English control. Walls and towers were constructed, encompassing both hills, but the castle was retaken and destroyed by Llywelyn ap Gruffyd (the Last) in 1263. When English control over Wales was finally established in 1284, Edward 1 decided to build a new castle across the river at Conwy. The few remains are largely those of Henry III's castle.

1 Go along Dale Road and at the junction turn RIGHT, then follow the road (Trinity Crescent) to crossroads. Turn RIGHT and follow the main road past North Wales Golf

Club and over the railway line, then turn LEFT up Hospital Road. After passing Maesdu Golf Club, take the next turning RIGHT (Ffordd yr orsedd) towards the entrance of Llandudno General Hospital. After 30 yards, turn RIGHT and follow the golf club car park perimeter fence to go through a kissing gate by a footpath post. Follow the hedge on your left between the hospital and the golf course, then go over a gap in a low shrub boundary, and continue up the left edge of a meadow alongside a fence – *enjoying good views.*

2 Near the fence corner, ignore a wooden stile just ahead. Instead, bear RIGHT to cross a footbridge over a stream then a ladder-stile. Go up the field edge, and on past a telegraph pole to go through shrubs in the field corner and over a ladder-stile. Go ahead for about 40 yards, then bear RIGHT up the slope to the top of an area of gorse and bramble. Continue ahead towards a telegraph pole and the tower, to cross a ladder-stile by a gate. Go up to the tower – *reputed to be one of a chain of coastal watchtowers built in the17th C to warn of possible invaders. There are great views of Anglesey, the Great Orme, Llandudno, along the coast, and down the Conwy valley to the Carneddau mountains. Nearby are the twin hills of Deganwy Castle.* Drop back down the slope then swing RIGHT down the field to cross a ladder-stile in the fence. Go half-LEFT to cross another ladder-stile. Keep ahead to cross a ladder-stile below farm buildings. Turn RIGHT and walk along the edge of three fields to reach a road by St. Hilary's church at Llanrhos. Turn RIGHT.

3 Take the next road on the right (Cae Rhos). Go past houses and through a kissing gate. Continue ahead, through another kissing gate, and on along a pathway between houses to emerge on a road. Go straight ahead along Hill View road, and at the T-junction turn RIGHT. Shortly, turn LEFT along the access lane to Maes Dalau farm/caravan park. Follow it as it bends right, then take the waymarked path between the side of a house and a long outbuilding. Go over a stile and along an old tree-lined

to walk △10

LLANDUDNO

West Parade

Golf Club

Hospital

N

West Shore

0   ¼ mile

tower

Llanrhos

Castle ruins

DEGANWY

Station

A546

Mostyn Estates). Turn LEFT along the fence towards the two small hills of Deganwy Castle, and at a building/sheep pens, bear half-RIGHT to go round the base of the first hill. Go across an area of level ground and follow a path up the left-hand side of the second hill. *On its summit are sparse ruins of Deganwy Castle and extensive views.* Return to the area of level ground and turn LEFT. Pass to the right of an isolated section of stonework, then bear half-LEFT to follow a path down and on past the northern base of the second hill, with the castle walls visible high up on its rocky slopes. About 60 yards from the house ahead, in line with two stones, swing LEFT to follow a clear path through the bracken beneath the hill's western slopes, passing just above houses to go through a kissing gate.

4 Follow a path to a road. Turn RIGHT and follow the road down to the A546 at Deganwy. Cross the road and take the waymarked path to the right of Deganwy Castle Hotel. Cross a bridge over the railway, go through the alleyway ahead, and turn RIGHT, then LEFT to reach a road by the Conwy estuary – *with views to Conwy Castle and across to the marina.* Turn RIGHT and follow a delightful coastal section of the North Wales Path along the promenade, close to the shoreline by sea defences, and through dunes back to the start – *enjoying fine views across to Conwy mountain, along the coast to Penmaenmawr, across to Anglesey and Puffin Island, and ahead to the Great Orme.*

green lane to cross a stile to enter the Vardre. Keep ahead up the large field to cross a ladder-stile in the top fence corner. Turn RIGHT and follow the fence to cross a stile in the fence corner. (*The next section is courtesy of*

About the author, David Berry

David has lived in North Wales for nearly 30 years and greatly appreciates the beauty, culture and history of its landscape. He hopes that his comprehensive guides will encourage people to explore its diverse scenery and rich heritage. A keen walker and photographer, with an interest in local history, he is equally at home on a country ramble or on a mountain top. He has also undertaken many long distance walks, including coast to coast crossings of Wales, Scotland and England.

WALK 12

BODLONDEB WOOD & CONWY MOUNTAIN

DESCRIPTION A 4½ mile walk (**A**) exploring part of the magnificent medieval walled town of Conwy with its imposing castle, a World Heritage Site, and its riverside and mountain setting, offering superb views throughout. The route features an exhilarating section of the old town wall, before passing along the tidal estuary of the river Conwy by attractive woodland. It then rises to complete a high-level circuit of the imposing Conwy Mountain, featuring an iron age hillfort at its highest point of 800 feet. Allow about 3 hours. The route includes an easy 1¼ mile walk (**B**) following a waymarked trail through Bodlondeb Wood, and a 3½ mile mountain walk (**C**) from Sychnant Pass described at the end.

START Mount Pleasant, by the western gateway, Conwy [SH 779776] or Sychnant Pass [SH 750770]

DIRECTIONS Follow the one-way system west through Conwy, past the Visitor's Centre, then after going through the old arched gateway, turn left into Mount Pleasant, where there is a pay and display car park. See **Walk 13** for the alternative start.

1 At the bottom of the car park by a stone shelter, go through a gap in the town walls into Upper Gate Street. Turn RIGHT and at the top of the road, go up the steps to gain access to the old town walls. *The walls, over ¾ mile in length, originally with 22 towers, were built in the 1280s at the same time as the castle by Edward I after his conquest of Wales, to enclose and protect the new town occupied by English settlers. The walls offer fine views inland to the mountains of Snowdonia, and over the town across the estuary to Deganwy.* Follow the town walls round down to their end for a good view along the quayside towards the castle and Telford's suspension bridge. Return to go down steps off the walls onto the road, and on the bend, swing RIGHT down Lower Gate Street then go LEFT past Shore cottage. Now follow Marine Walk along the shoreline of the estuary, with its many moored boats – *soon enjoying fine views across to Deganwy and the Great Orme. This delightful walkway was created by Albert Wood, one of Conwy's great benefactors, who entertained notable guests,*

such as Lloyd George, at the nearby Bodlondeb mansion, built for his family in 1877. All too soon, the walkway heads away from the estuary alongside Bodlondeb Wood.

2 For **Walk B**, just before the end of the wood, go through a gap in the wall and follow the waymarked path as it meanders through the wood. Eventually, it leaves the wood to drop down a meadow, then swings right along a pathway, passing beneath a greenhouse. Go past the Butterfly Jungle, and across the next pathway to go up a tarmaced path which you follow close by Bodlondeb, then bear left past toilets and follow the path signposted to the town centre.

For **Walk A** continue with the pathway – *with a first view of your destination: Conwy Mountain* – past the side of a school. At the road, turn LEFT and at a junction cross the main road and go straight ahead to cross a footbridge over the railway line. Continue along the edge of a wood, soon on a lane, and at a junction, bear RIGHT. Just beyond the end of the lane, follow the waymarked North Wales Path rising past cottages to go over a ladder-stile. Now you begin a steady ascent onto Conwy Mountain.

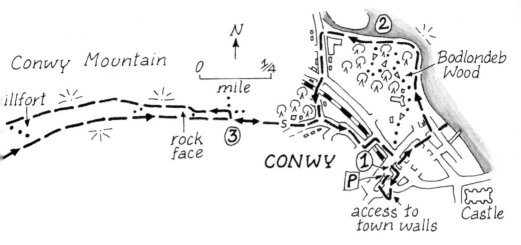

Conwy Mountain

illfort

rock face ③

CONWY ①

Bodlondeb Wood

access to town walls

Castle

0 ¼ mile

N

3 After a few hundred yards, at a waymark post by a large flat boulder – *with a good view looking back to Conwy castle* – turn RIGHT off the North Wales Path, and after 20 yards, at a cross-road of paths – *with good views looking across to the Great Orme, Llandudno and Deganwy* – turn LEFT on a path rising up the slope. *Just down to your right are the remains of a quarry which was once a source of millstone used for grinding flour.* At another path junction, with a small crag face just ahead, take the seaward path rising steadily up the bilberry, heather and bracken covered ridge – *enjoying excellent views on both sides: south to the part wooded Conwy valley and the fringes of the Carneddau mountains, and down to the Conwy marina, created after the building of the A55 tunnel under the river.* At the next path junction, go towards the rocky summit ahead. Keep with the path as it skirts the seaward side of the ridge, then at an easy access point, climb a few yards upon the ridge. Follow the ridge path to reach Castell Caer – *a late prehistoric hillfort, which once contained about 50 stone huts.* Continue along the edge of the fort and on with the main path, soon beginning a steady descent. At a distinct split in the path, take the RIGHT fork, then shortly take the next RIGHT fork to rejoin the North Wales Path at a waymark post.

4 Here, swing sharp LEFT and follow the waymarked path. It contours the mid-slopes of Conwy Mountain passing beneath Castell Caer, before making a gradual descent towards Conwy Castle, passing the rock face, popular with climbers, to join your outward path by the flat boulder at point **3**. Follow the path off the mountain, down the lane, then bear RIGHT along Mountain Road. At the junction, turn LEFT along Cadnant Park, go LEFT over the railway line, then RIGHT back to the start.

Walk C: from the top of the Sychnant Pass, take the waymarked North Wales Path along a track marked 'Private Road'. Just before a footpath post, turn RIGHT across stepping stones over the stream to avoid a wet area. Bear LEFT to go through a gateway, and on up the right fork of a stony track. Cross a green track and follow the North Wales Path round a small hill – *with good views across an old china-stone quarry to the Great Orme* – to join the main route at point **4**. Follow it to the flat boulder at point **3**, then turn LEFT to follow the higher route.

WALK 13

AROUND ALLTWEN & CWM GYRACH

DESCRIPTION A 5 mile walk (**A**) exploring the scenic hills and valleys around Sychnant Pass, with ever-changing views. The route leaves the top of the Pass to cross open hill country, passes an upland lake, before descending steeply, then more steadily, through attractive woodland into the valley and on to Capelulo, which offers a good choice of refreshments (inns, tea-shop, restaurant). It then climbs steadily on delightful green paths into open hill country to make a high-level circuit of the Gyrach valley, returning along a section of the way-marked North Wales Path. Allow about 3½ hours. The route offers described shorter options, and can easily be undertaken as a 2 mile walk (**B**) around Alltwen and a 4¼ mile high-level circuit (**C**) around Cwm Gyrach, using a delightful link path up the Sychnant Pass.

START Top of Sychnant Pass [SH 750770]

DIRECTIONS From Conwy follow signs for the Sychnant Pass. Follow the road up to the top of the Pass, and as the road begins to descend you will find off-road parking.

1 Take the waymarked North Wales Path along a track marked 'Private Road'. (*For* **Walk C** *follow a path down the dramatic side valley. Go past cottages, then follow the road to point* **3**.) Follow it past crags and round to a waymarked path junction. Here leave the North Wales Path and continue on the track towards a farm. Just before the entrance to Pen-prya, bear half-LEFT to follow a path alongside the wall. Go on past a small lake, where you bear half-LEFT. *Wild ponies graze in this area.* Shortly, when the path splits, take the less distinct LEFT fork. At another path junction, take the path descending towards trees – *with good views to Anglesey, Puffin Island and the shoreline.* Go down the right-hand edge of the forest on a short but steep descent.

2 At a level cross-path, turn LEFT to cross a ladder-stile. The delightful path now drops steadily through the attractive mixed woodland of Coed Pendryffryn. After about 200 yards, leave the main path to take a path on the left angling across an exposed small stony bank to a fence. Follow the fence along the edge of the wood – *with views up the slopes of Alltwen, on whose summit is an ancient hillfort* – past a ladder-stile. Keep on with the path just below the wood boundary, soon descending to swing RIGHT to a way-mark post, then LEFT past another post to drop down to join a broader level cross-path. Follow it LEFT to go through a kissing gate just beyond the end of the wood. Follow the path down to pass behind, then the front of, a row of terrace houses to cross a bridge over the river to reach Old Mill Road in Dwygyfylchi. Turn LEFT and follow the road alongside the river.

3 Just before the road crosses the river, take a waymarked path on the right. The stony path initially follows the river, then goes through woodland to reach Conwy Old road opposite Y Dwygyfylchi in the centre of Capelulo. *In the 18thC, Capelulo was an important coaching stop for travellers on the road through Sychnant Pass until a new coastal road was opened in the 1820s. Despite loss of the passing trade, it then became a popular place for Victorian visitors attracted to the beauty of the area.* (For **Walk B**, *follow the road left out of the village, then take the next road on the left. On the bend, turn right on a track by Llys Gwynt. Go past two more cottages, and keep straight ahead on the stony path rising up the valley with overhanging crags back to the start.*) For the **main route** go up the road opposite, past toilets. At a Snowdonia National Park sign keep ahead past cottages. (*For a shorter walk, turn left along a driveway over the river. Just before a house, take the signposted path on the left to begin a steady climb up the bracken-covered hillside to emerge at a wall corner. Continue ahead, then follow the wall on your right past a cottage. After passing a track, bear left to a waymark post to swing left with the North Wales Path.*) From Nant Uchaf continue up a stony track.

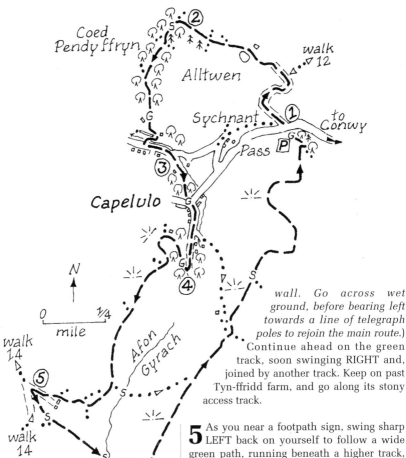

Coed
Pendyffryn

Alltwen

Sychnant

Pass

to Conwy

walk 12

Capelulo

N

0   ¼
       mile

walk 14

walk 14

Afon Gyrach

ruin

wall. *Go across wet ground, before bearing left towards a line of telegraph poles to rejoin the main route.)* Continue ahead on the green track, soon swinging RIGHT and, joined by another track. Keep on past Tyn-ffridd farm, and go along its stony access track.

5 As you near a footpath sign, swing sharp LEFT back on yourself to follow a wide green path, running beneath a higher track, to cross a ladder-stile over the wall. Now go LEFT to join the North Wales Path at a way-mark post. Follow the path to cross a foot-bridge over the Afon Gyrach – *a delightful place for a break.* Continue to a wall corner, then follow the wall on your right. At a ruin, go LEFT to follow the waymarked high-level North Wales Path across open country – *enjoying good open views. I have walked this route when the Lakeland fells were clearly visible!* At a crossroad of paths, keep with the North Wales Path – *with new views unfolding of Puffin island and western Anglesey* – now on a distinct track. When it bends right, go over the ladder-stile ahead and follow the North Wales Path – *enjoying ever changing views* – as it makes a steady descent back to the start.

4 At a track junction, swing RIGHT up through a gate, and on up the edge of woodland, soon on a delightful green track. At a waymarked path junction above a cottage, at a prominent viewpoint, keep on with the green track as it winds its way up the hillside. Eventually, it levels out in open countryside. Continue with the green track alongside a wall on your left, and when it splits, keep to the LEFT fork, still near the wall. (*For another shorter walk, cross an iron ladder-stile, go down the field edge, over a stile, and across the river. Go up the bank, then bear left on a path to walk alongside the*

DRUIDS CIRCLE & FOEL LUS

DESCRIPTION A 5-mile walk exploring the attractive hills and upland plateau above Penmaenmawr, featuring the famous Bronze Age Druids Circle and other ancient groups of stones, and an exhilarating high level panoramic walk around Foel Lus. After the initial steep ascent to reach the Circle standing at just over 1300 feet (400 m), the rest of the route offers delightful walking, with great views. Allow about 3½ hours. It can easily be shortened to a 4-mile walk, missing out the Foel Lus circuit if required.

START Car park by the library, Penmaenmawr.[SH 719763]

DIRECTIONS At the crossroad in the centre of Penmaenmawr go up Fernbrook road, signposted to the library, where there is a large car park on the right. This walk is also accessible by bus or train.

The hills and upland plateau above Penmaenmawr are rich in archaelogical evidence of early man. On the hill that towers above the town to the south, heavily scarred by quarrying, which continues to this day, is the site of Graiglwyd Neolithic axe factory – the 3rd largest production centre in Britain. Stone stronger than flint was first removed in blocks, then pieces flaked by hammerstone into rough shape, before being polished and attached to wooden handles. As Neolithic man began to settle on the land, axes were needed for clearing dense forest to create pasture, and building wooden houses. Axes made here have been found throughout Britain, indicating the existence of an extensive trading network. Later, partly encouraged by an improvement in climate, early Bronze Age man moved into the uplands, leaving behind an extensive range of burial and ritual monuments.

1 From the car park, turn RIGHT up the road and just past Y Berllan, go up a railed stepped pathway on the right. At its top turn RIGHT past houses, and at a road junction, swing LEFT. After 20 yards, bear RIGHT on a tarmac path past the side of Llys Machno into a road. Go ahead to a footpath post and on along an enclosed path, soon skirting round a ruin and on up a field to go through a kissing-gate onto a road. Follow it LEFT, then turn RIGHT up an access drive to a house and kennels on a path signposted to Druids Circle. Pass to the left of buildings, then at a corner wall, bear half-RIGHT up to go through a kissing gate. Now follow the path as it swings LEFT up the bracken covered hillside, passing a seat with a fine view. The path passes a small wood before climbing steadily up the edge of an attractive side valley. Strategically placed seats and excellent views assist in the increasingly steep climb. *Nearby to the west is the heavily quarried Graiglwyd mountain and site of the Neolithic axe factory.* After going over a long footbridge across a stream and reedy area, the path rises to go through a kissing gate in the wall. Go up the slope ahead to join the North Wales Path at a waymark post.

2 Here, turn RIGHT and follow the path west to reach a green track by a waymark post. Here, turn LEFT – *past the scant remains of a stone circle* – and follow this higher level route back across the mid-slopes, roughly parallel to the path just left. Soon you reach a more substantial stone circle on the edge of a plateau leading to Tal y Fan and grazed by wild ponies. A little further on is the Druids Circle – *an impressive large embanked stone circle dating from the 2nd millennium BC. which, in the 18thC was often sketched by travellers who passed by on the ancient mountain road below. It was probably originally used for rituals, then later for burials, as evidenced by the cremated remains of several young children found in its centre.* Drop down across a wettish gully and follow the clear path as it angles down to join the North Wales Path at a waymark post. Just to your right is the remains of another small stone circle.

3 Keep with the North Wales Path, passing a path junction, and on by a wall on your right – *soon with extensive views of the coast*

stretching from Llandudno, Conwy Mountain, and Little Orme to Rhyl/Prestatyn. The path then swings RIGHT through a gate and on down to bear LEFT along a tree-lined green track. Go pass Bryn Derwydd. To your right is a large glacial erratic stone – *Maen Crwn*. After going through a gate, keep on the track. In the field to your right is another stone circle. When the North Wales Path turns right through a gate, continue along the track. After going through a gate, the track bears LEFT to join another one.

4 About 80 yards after passing a side track, as the main track begins to descend, go half-RIGHT on a path through the heather. – *with dramatic views over Penmaenmawr across to Anglesey and Puffin Island. (For the shorter walk continue down the track.)* Soon, turn RIGHT along a cross path, and when you meet a stony track, follow it LEFT. Go past side tracks, and on alongside a good example of dry stone walling. At the wall corner, when the track bends down to a house, continue straight ahead on a green path, soon descending through heather

alongside telegraph poles – *with a superb view towards Conwy Mountain and the Great Orme, and Sychnant Pass.* At a path junction, by a seat, bear LEFT on the higher path to begin a superb section of path contouring round the steep slopes of Foel Lus – *created to celebrate Queen Victoria's Jubilee in 1887. Well placed seats allow you to stop to enjoy the great views – across Anglesey to Holyhead Mountain, and on a clear day north to the Lakeland fells.*

5 After passing through the 'gateway' to the Jubilee Path – go down the lane ahead. At an underground reservoir, go through a kissing gate opposite. Walk along the field edge, passing above a house, and on along a track, then cross a ladder-stile on the right opposite a small reservoir/fishery. Follow the path LEFT alongside the fence, passing between the end of the reservoir and a caravan site. Go through a kissing gate and on down a lane. At a road, turn LEFT and immediately bear RIGHT to follow an enclosed stony track/path to join your outward route by Llys Machno. Follow it back to the start.

1 From the bank, go LEFT back down the road, then take the first road on the right (Park Road), passing a small garage. Keep on Park Road past the Church Institute and modern houses/bungalows. When the road bears right, go through the iron gates ahead and along a rough track. When it splits, keep ahead on the stonier track – *enjoying fine views across to Anglesey and Puffin Island. Later, there are views looking back to Penrhyn Castle.* Follow the the track to a gate and continue along a lane. When it bends left by Bryn Goleu cottage, go half-RIGHT up a green track, through a gate, passing beneath a large black and white timber-framed house.

2 At the corner of the large boundary wall, swing RIGHT with the wall to go through a kissing gate, and on up through a wood. At a crossroad of paths, turn RIGHT and follow the stony path up through the wood. Soon the path bends sharp left, then at a path junction, turn RIGHT to go through a kissing gate. Continue ahead with the path, soon rising up a delightful narrow walled section. Go up steps and through a small gate by a house. Follow the waymarked path rising behind the house and a cottage. Just below a kissing gate, swing LEFT with the path – *enjoying great views across the Menai Straits* – up to go through another kissing gate. Follow the path up through the trees, soon bending RIGHT and continue up across open bracken-covered slopes – *offering superb views along the coast and inland to the mountains.* At a path junction by a solitary oak tree, turn LEFT. Soon bend RIGHT, and follow this delightful green path alongside an old boundary embankment up to go through a gap in the wall, and on up through a kissing gate by a clump of trees. Continue alongside the wall – *enjoying fine views to Tal-y-fan ahead, and towards Drum.*

3 At the wall corner, by a clump of conifers, continue ahead. (*For* **Walk B** *turn right and follow the wall down, past sheds by the bend of a quarry track, and on down through a kissing gate. Continue down past the end of a wood, over a stile by a cottage. Follow the wall down through the trees to go through a gate by the entrance to a house [Newry Cottage] and drop down onto a lane. Turn right and resume text at point* **5**.) Soon join and follow the quarry road. When it bends left, go through a kissing gate on the

28

right and follow the fence, then wall on your right into the wild open country towards the small rocky top of Clip yr Orsedd and the distant ridge of Tal-y-fan. Keep alongside the wall to follow a green track past a small part wall-enclosed rectangular pool and on

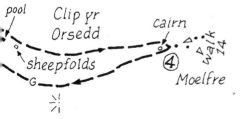

beneath the summit of Clip yr Orsedd. At sheepfolds, keep with the rising track angling away from the wall. It soon levels out and fades as it skirts the southern flanks of Clip yr Orsedd. It then runs beneath a line of telegraph posts to pass a collapsed stone-topped cairn, before dropping gently down to meet a green track beneath the flat-topped small hill of Moelfre. *Ahead on the skyline can be seen part of one of the area's stone circles. For an extension to the Druids Circle, continue ahead on the track, past the way-mark post and on up the small ridge. See* **Walk 14**.

4 Turn RIGHT along the green track. *Wild ponies graze on this upland landscape. Looking to the mountains to your left, the line of pylons mark the route of a Roman road.* The track soon begins a long and steady descent, following the waymarked North Wales Path, back to Llanfairfechan. It passes through a gate, then continues down alongside a fence, through another gate, and on down to pass by a cottage. Continue along its access track, past farm buildings, and after going through a gate by a quarry road, continue ahead down a shady lane, soon passing Newry Cottage. Follow the lane to a junction. Here, turn LEFT and continue down this quiet pleasant country road. When you reach a sharp bend by the entrance to

WALK 15
CLIP YR ORSEDD

DESCRIPTION A 6 mile walk (**A**) exploring the hills east of Llanfairfechan, with extensive views. The route rise in stages to pass through upland pasture grazed by wild ponies, reaching a height of over 1300 feet beneath the small rocky top of Clip yr Orsedd. It then follows the waymarked North Wales Path on a long and steady descent back to Llanfairfechan. Allow about 3½ hours. The route can easily be shortened to a 3¾ mile circuit (**B**) or extended to visit the Druids Circle.
START Llanfairfechan [SH 682747]
DIRECTIONS Turn off the A55 into Llanfairfechan. At the traffic lights by the shops, turn up Village Road, shortly signposted 'Town Hall/Post Office/Library'. Turn right by the HSBC bank, just before the school, to a small car park behind the bank.

Nant y Coed Nature Reserve, follow the North Wales Path across a footbridge over the Afon Llanfairfechan to a road. Follow it RIGHT, past a side road and on a gentle descent. Keep with the road, after the North Wales Path leaves it.

5 At the far end of Bron Cae cottages – *with a good view overlooking Llanfairfechan* – go half-RIGHT down a rough lane. Keep ahead at a junction, to the lane's end by two houses, then follow a tarmac path along the edge of a golf course. After dropping down a handrailed section of path, bear LEFT along a wide tarmac pathway between houses. Cross a road by a telephone box, and go down the lane ahead, past a side road, and along a pathway to emerge on Llannerch road. Turn RIGHT, past a side road to go up past a churchyard. Shortly, go through a kissing gate on the left by Gwesty Pen-y-Bryn. Follow the enclosed path behind the pub and by the church, and on down to cross a footbridge over the river, to almost unexpectedly arrive back at your starting point.

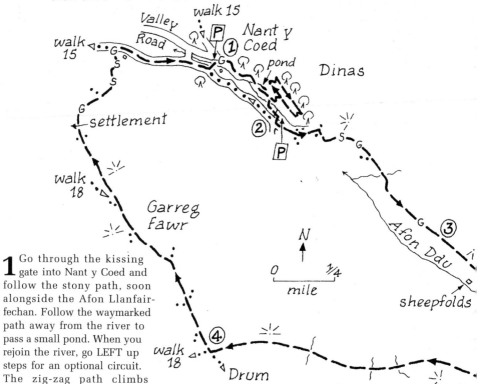

LLANFAIRFECHAN

walk 15

Valley Road

Nant y Coed

Dinas

pond

walk 15

settlement

walk 18

Garreg Fawr

N

0   ¼
mile

Afon Ddu

sheepfolds

walk 18

Drum

1 Go through the kissing gate into Nant y Coed and follow the stony path, soon alongside the Afon Llanfairfechan. Follow the waymarked path away from the river to pass a small pond. When you rejoin the river, go LEFT up steps for an optional circuit. The zig-zag path climbs through the trees. At a path junction keep ahead and follow the delightful path up across the attractive oak and scree covered steep slopes, before descending on the panoramic return route. After rejoining the riverside path, cross the river by large stepping stones, and go through a kissing gate. Follow the fence on your left upriver and on through a small field. Go through a kissing gate, over more stepping stones and up a stepped path to emerge into a car park.

2 On leaving the car park, turn LEFT along the lower of two tracks. (*For* **Walk B**, *turn right along the road. At a bend, go right over a footbridge.*) Go through a kissing gate and follow the track, soon crossing over the river. Keep with the RIGHT fork of the track, rising past a waymark post. After about 40 yards, go LEFT off the track and follow the waymarked path up the edge of a side valley. *Up to your left are the scree-covered slopes*

of Dinas, part of the nearby Graiglwyd Neolithic axe factory (See **Walk 14***). On its top is an Iron Age hillfort containing remains of hut circles.* At a track keep ahead up the waymarked path, and follow it round up to cross a stile – *with views looking back across to Anglesey.* Follow the path by a reedy stream to go through a kissing gate. Continue ahead, soon following a green track up the stone covered hillside. It soon levels out, crosses a stream, then bends towards the side valley, before climbing up the hillside again. At its end go through a kissing gate. *Ahead is a panorama of mountains.* Go ahead for 20 yards, then bear half-LEFT up a path to pass round the left-hand edge of an area of reeds onto a small rise.

3 Now continue ahead across the gorse and boulder covered upland pasture, *grazed by sheep and wild ponies*, towards a group of distant pylons at Bwlch y

Ddeufaen, lying between the ridges of Foel Lwyd and Drosgl. *The sheepfolds you see are of a type unique to the Carneddau area. They were used by farmers to sort out the ownership of sheep rounded up from the open hills.* Work your way towards the middle/nearest of the cluster of three pylons. Pass just beneath the pylon and on over a ladder-stile in the wall ahead. Follow a path ahead – *soon with a standing stone by a pylon visible on your right* – to drop down to a more impressive standing stone by the ancient trackway. *According to legend these stones were dropped by a female giant on route to Ireland.* Follow the track up past the other standing stone and cross a ladder-stile at the top of Bwlch y Ddeufaen (*the pass of the two stones*). Continue along the track. *Do not let the pylons detract from your enjoyment of this wild upland landscape. As you stretch your legs, reflect on the historical importance of this ancient highway. Pre-historic man walked this way, then the Romans used this line for their paved road which ran from Canovium fort in the Conwy Valley to Segontium in Caernarfon. Later, drovers followed this mountain road with their cattle. Ahead, running across the slopes is the track leading up to Drum.*

4 After about 1¼ miles you reach a waymarked path junction, known as 'The meeting of the tracks' – with the optional extension to Drum. Here, turn RIGHT towards Llanfairfechan, soon joining a green track. Follow it down to a junction of paths. Keep straight ahead and follow the way-marked North Wales Path, soon on a steady descent across the slopes of Garreg Fawr – enjoying panoramic views over the coast to Anglesey. *This delightful green track provides a superb finale to the mountain walk from the Gower to Snowdonia.* Where the track splits by a wall, keep ahead with the North Wales Path and on down the gorse covered hillside to a waymark post at a crossroad of tracks. *Visible below is the remains of an old enclosed hut settlement.* Continue ahead down to go through a kiss-

WALK 16

NANT Y COED & BWLCH Y DDEUFAEN

DESCRIPTION A 5½ mile walk **(A)** through the delightful wooded valley of Nant y Coed Nature Reserve and up across the wild high upland pastures and moorland above Llanfairfechan, featuring pre-historic sites, an ancient mountain highway, and panoramic views. The route explores Nant y Coed, popular with visitors since the late 19thC., then rises steadily across open country to reach two Bronze Age standing stones, situated at nearly 1400 feet by an ancient trackway, later a Roman Road, at Bwlch y Ddeufaen. It follows this ancient trackway, skirting beneath the northern Carneddau mountains to a once important crossroad of tracks. From here you could extend the walk to Drum (2528 feet) on a clear track, adding 4¼ miles to the distance. The route then follows the North Wales Path on a delightful green track down across Garreg Fawr, with superb views. Allow about 3½ hours. The route offers an easy 1 mile circuit of Nant y Coed **(B)**.

START Entrance to Nant y Coed, Llanfairfechan [SH 695740].

DIRECTIONS Turn off the A55 into Llanfairfechan. At traffic lights by shops, turn up Village Road, passing the school. At a junction, turn left along Bryn Road and on along Valley Road. After the last houses continue ahead up Newry Drive to reach a small parking area on the bend by Nant y Coed Information board.

ing gate. Follow the delightful green path angling down the hillside – *with good views overlooking Llanfairfechan* – past a seat and a side path to cross a ladder-stile. Go down between two boundaries, over a ladder-stile, then bear LEFT across a field to reach a road. Turn RIGHT along the road, past a side turning, and on a bend go half-LEFT – *with the North Wales Path over a footbridge to the start.*

*T*raeth Lafan lying between Llanfair-fechan and Bangor, is a designated Site of Special Scientific Interest and a Special Protection area. It attracts huge flocks of birds, including many species of wildfowl and wading birds during spring and autumn migration, and large numbers of overwintering waders. The sand, shingle, saltmarsh and extensive mudflats exposed at low tide stretching over towards Anglesey, offer an abundance of food – ie. ragworms, snails, cockles, and mussels, as well as fish - that attract and sustain a wide variety of birds. These include redshank, oystercatcher, shellduck, teal, wigeon, mallard, the great-crested grebe, merganser, goldeneye, lapwing, and curlew.

There are no fewer than four designated nature reserves linked by a coastal path – the Spinnies at Aber

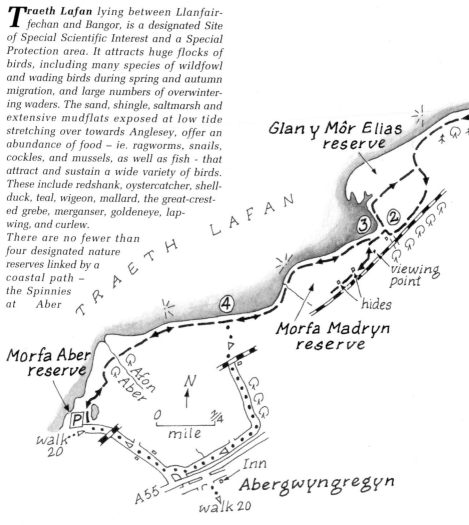

Ogwen, Morfa Aber, Morfa Madryn – all containing hides for discreet viewing of birds – and the open saltmarsh reserve of Glan y Mor Elias.

1 Walk west along the promenade and over the river where it joins the sea to a wooden shelter, displaying information on birds that you might see. Follow the shoreline pathway, passing a small lake to join another pathway by houses. Continue along the tarmac pathway above the rocky shore – *enjoying views across to Puffin Island and*

Anglesey, and along the coast to Penrhyn Castle and Bangor pier, and inland to the northern Carneddau range of mountains. You pass an area of mixed woodland, with a slate perimeter fence – *a feature of this area – to reach Glan y Mor Elias Nature Reserve. At the seaward side of the saltmarsh is a shingle ridge and spit known locally as 'Shell Island', where oystercatchers and ringed plover roost. Access is restricted during March to August, or at high tide, to avoid disturbance. Continue along the pathway, soon bending away from the shore. Follow*

32

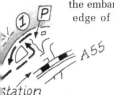

Station
LANFAIRFECHAN

the embanked green path round the edge of the saltmarsh reserve to run close to the railway line.

2 At the corner of the reserve by an information board, cross a stream by a house, and bear RIGHT to reach Morfa Madryn Nature Reserve – *consisting of landscaped shallow pools and low lying marshy fields.* From the information board follow a path alongside the reserve perimeter and on to reach the further of two hides for a viewing of the birds. 75 yards further along the path is an unusual stone memorial to two racehorses – *Kingsford (1922–32) and Kinnaird (1920–31), the winner of 22 and 19 races respectively.* Retrace your steps, and after the path bends towards the shore, go up steps on your right to a viewing area looking over the reserve, then return to the reserve entrance by a choice of paths.

3 For **Walk B** return to the Glan y Mor Elias information board, then turn LEFT along the grassy bank overlooking the mudflats. Just before an inlet, swing RIGHT along the grass embankment – *giving excellent views of birds feeding on the saltmarsh and in the deep channels which bisect it* – to join your outward path. Follow it back to Llanfairfechan. Go round the right hand side of the lake back to the start – *passing an interesting old plaque in the wall reflecting a different era of users of this walkway at the beginning of the 20thC.*

For **Walk A** follow the coastal path west towards Penrhyn Castle It passes behind a stone wall and on between fences. Just before its end, drop down onto the beach and continue alongside the stone wall.

4 At its corner you have a choice. For the direct route to Morfa Aber Reserve simply continue with the coastal path. (*For the inland route, turn left and follow an old green lane away from the shore. Cross the main railway line, taking heed of the warn-*

WALK 17
TRAETH LAFAN NATURE RESERVES

DESCRIPTION This 6 mile **(A)** walk is a delight for birdwatchers. It features visits to three coastal nature reserves, lying alongside the unspoilt Traeth Lafan (Lavan Sands), internationally renowned for its birdlife. The route, which can be accessed by train, visits Glan y Mor Elias and Morfa Madryn nature reserves, then extends to Morfa Aber reserve by using the coast path for the outward and return route, or by combining it with lanes to include a refreshment stop at the Aber Falls Hotel. Allow 3 hours plus time for birdwatching. The route includes a shorter 3 mile circuit **(B)** visiting the first two reserves. The coastal path from Llanfairfechan to Morfa Madryn is on tarmac then grass, suitable for strong wheelchairs, after which it varies from grass to shingle and pebble. Binoculars are recommended. Keep dogs under strict control and away from any flocks of birds. Where possible, time your walk to avoid high tide in order not to disturb birds roosting on the narrow upper shore.

START Promenade, Llanfairfechan [SH 679754]

DIRECTIONS At traffic lights in the centre of Llanfairfechan, turn down Station Road, go under the railway by the nearby station, to reach a large car park with toilets and cafe by the promenade.

ing signs, then follow a road to a junction at Abergwyngregyn. For refreshments at the nearby Aber Falls Hotel go under the A55. Otherwise, turn right, and right again at the next junction. Shortly, take a side road to reach Morfa Aber Reserve.) If you are feeling energetic, you could extend the walk to Aber Ogwen! For either route, simply follow the coast path back to Morfa Madryn, then continue with **Walk B** through Glan y Mor Elias Reserve back to the start.

WALK 18

GARREG FAWR FROM ABER

DESCRIPTION A 6-mile walk exploring the foothills of the Carneddau range between Abergwyngregyny and Llanfairfechan, rich in remains of pre-historic settlement and burial sites, and offering contrasting mountain and coastal views. The route rises from the wooded side valley of Cwm Anafon up onto open upland pasture reaching a height of over 800 feet, before descending in stages towards Llanfairfechan. It then follows delightful paths up to pass by Garreg Fawr to reach an important crossroad of tracks at over 1279 feet, where there is an option to extend the walk to Drum (2528 feet) on a clear track, adding 4¼ miles to the walk. The route returns along an ancient trackway, once a Roman road, on a section of the North Wales Path. Allow about 4 hours.
START Bont Newydd, Abergwyngregyny [SH 662720]
DIRECTIONS See **Walk 19**.

1 Go across Bont Newydd (the new bridge), built in the 1820s, and follow the road rising steadily up the eastern edge of the densely wooded side valley above Afon Anafon for about ½ mile. After passing under power cables, cross a stone stile on the left by a footpath post. Follow a path up through the bracken to pass the right hand edge of a small clump of trees. Here go half-LEFT to follow a faint path angling up across the bracken-covered hillside to reach a level path just to the left of the base of large pylon. Turn LEFT and immediately go half-RIGHT up through the bracken, past a small tree, over a cross-path, and on for a further 20 yards to reach a higher cross-path by a crab-apple tree. Follow it LEFT across the bracken and gorse covered slopes – *soon looking beyond the valley to Anglesey.*

2 Keep on with the main path across more open slopes towards a boundary wall. When the path splits near a boulder, keep on the RIGHT fork, and just beyond an isolated

tree, again follow the RIGHT fork up the hillside. About 40 yards before the large boundary wall, swing RIGHT up to cross a ladder-stile on the skyline – *with good views looking back.* Continue ahead – *soon looking down over Llanfairfechan to the sea* – then follow the wall on your left down the field, and cross a ladder-stile in the corner – *with Puffin Island now visible.* Continue down the next field edge to go over an iron ladder-stile. Keep ahead down the large field, through a reedy area and on to join the boundary wall. Follow it down to cross a ladder-stile in the field corner, then drop down to a cross-path in the trees. Turn RIGHT and almost immediately turn LEFT to follow a path down through an area of rhododendrum and trees to cross stepping stones over the river. Ignore a path leading left alongside the river.

Instead, follow the path ahead up through the trees to go through a kissing gate. Head half-LEFT across the field – *with good views across to Beaumaris* – to go over a ladder-stile onto a lane. Follow it LEFT.

3 After about 100 yards, on the bend by a telegraph pole, go RIGHT up a path and through a kissing gate. Now follow the fence on your left down and round beneath the bracken-covered hillside to go through a gate by a house. Continue along a green track, through another gate and on ahead along the nearby farm's access track – *enjoying good views across Traeth Lafan to Anglesey, and to the west, near Bangor, Penrhyn Castle clearly visible* – over a cattle grid and on to reach a road. Follow it east, and soon, at a road junction by a ruin bearing a Llanerch road sign, turn RIGHT up the road.

4 At an old farmhouse, turn RIGHT over a ladder-stile and follow the attractive enclosed track, featuring a band of exposed rock as a base, up to go through a kissing gate. Continue with the green track, and after about 150 yards, it climbs away from the

wall up the gorse covered hillside. It bends left to accompany another wall, then right to rise steadily up the hillside. Soon leave the green track by the wall to follow a nearby parallel path through the gorse which leads to the North Wales Path. *Keep looking back to enjoy the superb views from Llanfairfechan to Bangor.* Follow it RIGHT past a waymark post and on with a green track alongside the wall. At its corner, when the track splits, keep with the North Wales Path, which rises steadily up the slopes of Garreg Fawr, and on to pass to the left of a pylon to reach a way-marked crossroad of paths, known as 'The meeting of the tracks' – Rowen, Drum, Aber and Llanfairfechan – at the northern end of the Carneddau mountains.

5 Turn RIGHT and follow the track on a steady descent westwards towards Aber. *You are now walking along the Roman road* based on a pre-historic mountain trackway, which ran from Canovium fort in the Conwy Valley, up through Bwlch y Daufaen just to the east, to Segontium in Caer-narfon. Evidence of its original paving has been found. It later became an important drover's route, with Aber serving as a stopping station. Man has long been associated with this wild upland landscape, as evidenced by the many pre-historic burial and settlement sites it contains. Traditionally, these upland pastures were grazed by cattle during the summer, but by the early 19thC, sheep had taken over as the dominant economy. Wild ponies still graze here. After a while, the track swings south down towards a densely forest-ed mountainside in Cwm Anafon, then bends again to go through a gate. Pass through a small rough parking area and on along the road, which then descends the side of the valley, soon on your outward route back to the start.

WALK 19

COEDYDD ABER

DESCRIPTION A 5¾ mile (**A**) walk through the Coedydd Aber National Nature Reserve, featuring the stunning Aber Falls (Rhaedr Fawr) in its magnificent mountain setting, and an exploration of open upland pasture following a highly scenic section of the North Wales Path, with extensive views. The route takes the popular trail to Aber Falls, then passes another waterfall, before making a steady ascent across open slopes. It then crosses the hills overlooking the coast, before descending a side valley and following field paths to Abergwyngregyny. Allow about 3½ hours. The route includes a shorter 3¾ mile (**B**) walk and a simple 2½ mile circuit (**C**) to Aber Falls.

START Bont Newydd, Abergwyngregyny [SH 662720]

DIRECTIONS Turn off the A55 signposted to Abergwyngregyny, and follow the signs for Aber Falls, passing through the village and along the wooded valley road to reach parking areas just before the road crosses the river (Bont Newydd). Alternatively, go over the bridge, then turn right to reach a Forestry Enterprise car park/ toilets. (From here, walk back along the lane, go across a footbridge over the river, then bear right on the waymarked Aber Falls path up through the trees and on along a track to join the main route by an information board.)

*C*oedydd Aber, *managed by the Countryside Council for Wales, is located in a steep-sided valley between the Carneddau mountains and the coastal plain. Extensive archaeological remains, including pre-historic burial and settlement sites, reveal man's association with this sheltered valley and surrounding uplands for over 3000 years. Its dense mixed woodland is now the home of both woodland and mountain birds. The famous waterfall, formed during the Ice Age, has attracted visitors since the late 18th C, aided by the opening of the post road in the 1820's and the railway in 1848. The river rises as Yr Afon Goch (red river) and flows over the 100 foot rock face to become Afon* Rhaedr Fawr *(the river of the great falls) which flows down to the sea. It is one of the steepest rivers from source to mouth in England and Wales.*

1 Go through the kissing gate by an information board near Bont Newydd (the new bridge) built in the 1820s. Follow the path alongside the river. After crossing a footbridge over the river, go on through a kissing gate, then turn RIGHT along a stony track. Keep with the main track signposted to the waterfall, as it climbs steadily up the increasingly open wooded valley, soon giving views to the mountains ahead, to reach Nant Rhaedr. *This was originally a Welsh tyddyn (smallholding), which once sold tea and home-made lemonade to Victorian visitors on route to the Falls, and now contains an exhibition.* Continue along the track, later becoming a path, and, suddenly, the impressive waterfall comes into view. Go through a kissing gate and on to reach the base of the waterfall.

2 Retrace your steps, and for **Walk A**, cross the footbridge over the river. (*For* **Walk C**, *return to the kissing gate, cross the nearby ladder-stile, and follow the waymarked path angling up the rocky slope to enter the forest. Follow the path through the forest, then alongside its boundary to rejoin your outward route.*) Follow the path up above the river to cross a ladder-stile and continue on the waymarked North Wales Path, as it crosses the bracken and boulder strewn slopes, soon alongside a wall, beneath impressive crags. Cross a footbridge over another river, beneath another waterfall. Follow the path over several streams then a ladder-stile. At a waymark post, go half-RIGHT with the North Wales Path, soon crossing a stream. The path now rises, then crosses the open slopes. After crossing a ladder-stile continue up the delightful green track, over two further stiles, and under electricity cables. Soon the track makes a gentle descent – *with new views to Anglesey, Puffin Island and east along the coast to the Great Orme* – then levels out between two further stiles, before passing two barns. Cross a ladder-stile at a prominent viewpoint looking down to the coast.

36

3 Here the track splits. Take the LEFT fork, still on the North Wales Path. (*For* **Walk B**, *follow the other stony*

track down the hillside. At a waymark post turn right, and follow a path angling down the steep slope to reach the road.) Follow the green track through a narrow strip of plantation and on to cross a ladder-stile. Continue ahead on a rougher track by the fence – *enjoying extensive views of Anglesey, and the coast from the Great Orme to Bangor. Clearly visible are Bangor pier and Penrhyn Castle.* Cross another ladder-stile and follow the level track as it continues across the open slopes. After crossing another ladder-stile, keep ahead with the track passing above a steep side valley.

4 Just before the next ladder-stile, swing RIGHT with the green track down the hillside, and across a stream. After going through a gateway into a field, leave the track and go down the left field edge. After about 50 yards, drop down to follow the stream down through the trees to cross a ladder-stile by a cottage. Go on down its access track, and after about 100 yards, at a waymark post in the roots of a large tree, turn RIGHT up the bank. Go across the field, over a ladder-stile ahead, and on over another stile to pass above farm buildings. Soon drop down through the trees to go through a gate at the end of the outbuildings. Continue ahead between the side of the house and another building to go through a small gate

into a field. Follow a green track up to cross a stile. Continue ahead, and at the bend of another track, follow it down to go through a kissing gate by cottages, and on over a ladder-stile ahead. Go across the field and through a kissing gate. Keep ahead, through another kissing gate, and on across the bracken-covered slopes overlooking Abergwyngregyny, past a seat, and on down across the hillside. Go through a kissing gate and on alongside a fence, to drop down through a gate onto the road. Turn RIGHT and follow the road back to the start.

WALK 20
TRAETH LAFAN & FOOTHILLS

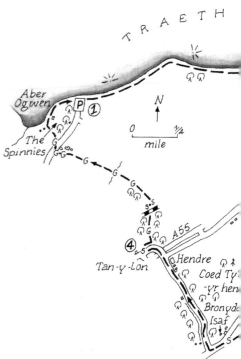

DESCRIPTION From Aber Ogwen, near Bangor, this 7½ mile walk, offering extensive birdlife and great views, follows the coastal path east for 3 miles along the unspoilt shoreline of Traeth Lafan (see **Walk 17**) to Morfa Aber nature reserve, before heading inland to Abergwyngregyny, where refreshments are available at the Aber Falls Hotel. It then ascends the hillside to follow the scenic high-level North Wales Path across the open slopes of the northern Carneddau foothills, before descending on quiet roads, passing Hendre, a preserved Victorian farm/tearoom, and on with field paths to The Spinnies nature reserve. Allow about 4½ hours. A shorter, lower level alternative to the North Wales Path section is to follow quiet lanes from Aber. Binoculars are recommended. Keep dogs under strict control and away from any flocks of birds. Where possible, time your walk to avoid high tide in order not to disturb birds roosting on the narrow upper shore.

START Aber Ogwen car park. [SH 616724]

DIRECTIONS From Bangor, turn off the A5122 by Penrhyn Castle towards Tal-y-Bont, passing over the river. Ignore turnings into Tal-y-Bont, then take a road on the left, signposted 'Nature Reserve'. Go past the reserve to the shore car park at the road end.

1 Head east from the car park to follow the coastal path along the shingle shoreline – with views across to Beaumaris and Puffin island. *As you pass round beneath small cliffs, new views unfold along the coast to the Great Orme.* The path then continues on grass past a small wood, and on alongside an attractive slate boundary. Follow the grassy embankment to its end, then continue along the rocky shore. *In 1648, this area was the scene of a battle, known as Y Dalar Hir (the long front) which saw Parliamentarian troops defeat Royalist forces.* After crossing a stream, go up onto a grass embankment to soon join an access track by a house. *Prior to* the building of Telford's suspension bridge over the Menai Straits in 1826, crossing to and from the mainland was hazardous. Mail and travellers to Anglesey and Ireland were ferried from near here to Beaumaris. Cattle would be driven across Traeth Lafan when the channel was at its narrowest, risking quicksand and the ravages of the fast incoming tide. Follow the track to Morfa Aber reserve.

2 Go along the road, passing under the railway. At a junction, continue up the road. At the next junction, turn LEFT towards Abergwyngregyny to pass under the A55. Turn LEFT (for the low level lane alternative turn right). *Originally the village was known as Aber Garth, but was later changed to Aber-gwyngregyn (the estuary of the white shells). It was a favourite manor of the Princes of Gwynedd in the 13thC. According to legend, it was here that Llywelyn the Great imprisoned his wife Joan, the daughter of*

3 When the track bends right down towards the coast, go over the ladder-stile ahead. Follow the fence on your right, past a pylon, and on over a ladder-stile by a stream. Keep on with the level green track, crossing two further stiles. The track now makes a long gentle swing down towards the coast, then bends round to cross a ladder-stile, before continuing across the open slopes parallel to the coast. After crossing a ladder-stile by a forest corner, follow the track down to a lane by Bronydd Isaf. Turn LEFT. Go down the lane, and at a junction, turn RIGHT and follow the road down the attractive wooded valley and on to reach Hendre – *built in 1860 for the Penrhyn estate for horse breeding and training.* Follow the road down and across the A55.

4 Just before a junction at Tan-y-Lon, cross a stile on the right, by a footpath post. Bear RIGHT and follow the concrete track round to its end. Continue ahead along a green track, through a wood, under a railway line and over a stile into a field. Go half-RIGHT to cross a ladder-stile, then turn LEFT to walk along the field edge. Go through a kissing gate at the end of a small wood, then go straight across the next field and through a gate in the boundary ahead. Follow the boundary on your right and on with a track – *with Penrhyn Castle, built between 1819-35 from wealth accrued from the slate industry,* prominent on the skyline – to pass farm buildings. Follow the waymarked path through a gate, passing to the left of the house to a road. Turn RIGHT to reach the entrance to The Spinnies nature reserve. Follow the path through the reserve to the hide to watch the birds on the lagoon, then gain access to the nearby Ogwen estuary. Turn RIGHT and follow the shoreline back to the start.

England's King John, and hanged William de Breos, Prince of Powys after discovering their *affair.* Shortly, with Aber Falls Hotel ahead, turn RIGHT, signposted Aber Falls. Take the next turning RIGHT. Go through the village, past two left turnings, and just past Nant-y-Felin, go up steps and through a small gate on the right by a footpath post. After 25 yards, take the LEFT fork rising steeply up the hillside to cross a stile. *Here are extensive views over Traeth Lafan and along the coast from the Great Orme to Bangor.* Continue up towards a plantation. At a waymark post, turn LEFT up a stony track to another waymark post just before a stile. Here, swing RIGHT along a green track on the waymarked North Wales Path to pass through a strip of forest and on to cross a stile. Follow the high-level track as it crosses open upland pasture, crossing two further stiles – *enjoying superb views.* Keep on with the track passing above a steep side valley.

PRONUNCIATION

These basic points should help non-Welsh speakers

Welsh	English equivalent
c	always hard, as in cat
ch	as in the Scottish word lo**ch**
dd	as th in **then**
f	as v in **v**ocal
ff	as **f**
g	always hard as in got
ll	no real equivalent. It is like 'th' in **then**, but with an 'L' sound added to it, giving '**thlan**' for the pronunciation of the Welsh 'Llan'.

In Welsh the accent usually falls on the last-but-one syllable of a word.

KEY TO THE MAPS

— →   Walk route and direction

    Metalled road

    Unsurfaced road

••••   Footpath/route adjoining walk route

~~→   River/stream

♣ ۿ   Trees

▄▄▄   Railway

G   Gate

S   Stile

F.B.   Footbridge

☀   Viewpoint

P   Parking

T   Telephone

🚐   Caravan site

THE COUNTRY CODE

Enjoy the countryside and respect its life and work

Guard against all risk of fire

Leave gates *as you find them*

Keep your dogs under close control

Keep to public paths across farmland

Use gates and stiles to cross fences, hedges and walls

Leave livestock, crops and machinery alone

Take your litter home

Help to keep all water clean

Protect wildlife, plants and trees

Take special care on country roads

Make no unnecessary noise

I wish to give particular thanks to Conwy and Denbighshire Countryside Services, Conwy County Borough Council Highways Department, BHP Petroleum, Mostyn Estates and the Snowdonia National Park Area Warden, for their invaluable advice and assistance.

Published by
Kittiwake
3 Glantwymyn Village Workshops,
Cemmaes Road, Machynlleth, Montgomeryshire
SY20 8LY

© Text & map research: David Berry 2002
© Maps: Kittiwake 2002

Cover photographs by David Berry – large: The Great Orme from Conwy Mountain (Walk **12**); inset: Point of Ayr lighthouse (Walk **1**).

Printed by WPG, Welshpool, Powys

ISBN: 1 902302 18 4